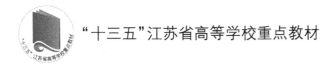

"十三五"江苏省高等学校重点教材

Intercultural Communication and Etiquette

跨文化交际与礼仪

主　编　朱建新　刘玉君
副主编　孙建光　陈晓靖　余洪红　李景光
编　委　顾荣荣　李　梓　杨　苏　李　辉

东南大学出版社
SOUTHEAST UNIVERSITY PRESS
·南京·

内容提要

本教材首先介绍了跨文化交际研究涉及的"文化""交际""跨文化交际"等核心概念、特点及其关系,随后从中西方文化产生差异的哲学根源对中西方价值观进行对比,使学生从根本上了解中西文化差异的根源,帮助其建立民族文化自信以及消除文化自我中心主义。在此基础之上编者通过案例列举了文化差异在言语和非言语交际方面的种种表现,讨论英汉语言背后的文化原因,并从中西文化对比的角度概述不同文化中的社会习俗以及在跨文化交际中我们需要掌握的礼仪。在最后的补充阅读部分,列举了部分"一带一路"沿线国家的风俗和礼仪,以帮助学生了解多样化的文化风俗和礼仪,拓展学生的跨文化视野,亦可作为学生日后进行外事交流时的重要参考。

图书在版编目(CIP)数据

跨文化交际与礼仪/朱建新,刘玉君主编. —南京:东南大学出版社,2019.2(2024.1重印)
ISBN 978-7-5641-8224-3

Ⅰ.①跨… Ⅱ.①朱… ②刘… Ⅲ.①文化交流—研究—中国、西方国家 Ⅳ.①G125

中国版本图书馆 CIP 数据核字(2018)第 298703 号

责任编辑:刘 坚　　责任校对:张万莹　　封面设计:王 玥　　责任印制:周荣虎

跨文化交际与礼仪 Kuawenhua Jiaoji Yu Liyi

主　　编	朱建新　刘玉君
出版发行	东南大学出版社
社　　址	南京市四牌楼2号　邮编:210096　电话:025-83793330
网　　址	http://www.seupress.com
电子邮箱	press@seupress.com
经　　销	全国各地新华书店
印　　刷	广东虎彩云印刷有限公司
开　　本	787 mm×1092 mm　1/16
印　　张	12.25
字　　数	300千字
版　　次	2019年2月第1版
印　　次	2024年1月第6次印刷
书　　号	ISBN 978-7-5641-8224-3
定　　价	40.00元

本社图书若有印装质量问题,请直接与营销部联系,电话:025-83791830。

前　言

随着全球经济一体化程度的不断加深,世界各国之间的交流日益频繁。各种不同文化间的相互影响、碰撞乃至融合日渐增多。不同文化背景的人们如何能够顺利地进行交流,如何培养和造就出更多的适应当前国家需要、通晓不同文化的复合型人才正成为新时代高等教育面临的共同课题。《国家中长期教育改革与发展纲要(2010—2020年)》指出:"我们必须培养大批具有国际视野、通晓国际规则、能够参与国际事务和国际竞争的国际化人才。"因此,进一步提高大学生对本民族的文化自信,增强其对异域文化的了解,使其成为既懂专业又具有较高跨文化交际能力的国际化人才,满足社会发展的迫切需求已经是当代高等教育的主要任务之一。

《大学英语教学指南》中提出将大学英语课程设置为通用英语、专门用途英语和跨文化交际三类课程,将跨文化交际首次正式纳入大学英语课程。《跨文化交际与礼仪》即是在任课老师积累了多年教学经验的基础上编写的一本适合"应用型"本科院校学生使用的教材,以供此类高校中达到大学英语教学要求中"较高要求"或"更高要求"层次的学生使用,旨在提高学生的跨文化意识和跨文化交际能力。

本教材编写思路明晰,语言浅显易懂。本教材首先介绍了跨文化交际研究涉及的"文化""交际""跨文化交际"等核心概念、特点及其关系,随后从中西方文化产生差异的哲学根源对中西方价值观进行对比,使学生从根本上了解中西文化差异的根源,帮助其建立民族文化自信以及消除自我文化中心主义。在此基础之上编者通过案例列举了文化差异在言语和非言语交际方面的种种表现,讨论英汉语言背后的文化原因,并从中西文化对比的角度概述不同文化中的社会习俗,以及在跨文化交际中我们需要掌握的礼仪。在最后的补充阅读部分,列举了部分"一带一路"沿线国家的风俗和礼仪,以帮助学生了解多样化的文化风俗和礼仪,扩大学生的跨文化视野,亦可作为学生日后进行外事交流时的重要参考。练习编写从学生学习的实际需求出发,从关键词汇的掌握,到阅读理解能力的提高,通过案例的分析、个人展示、话题讨论等培养学生的批判性思维,力求师生能在教与学的过程中教学相长。

《跨文化交际与礼仪》由朱建新、刘玉君主编,编委成员有孙建光、陈晓靖、余洪红、李景光、顾荣荣、李梓、杨苏和李辉等。在教材编写的过程中,得到了各位评审专家的指点,东南大学出版社的编审刘坚博士后也提出了许多建设性的意见,在此我们一并表达衷心的谢意。此外,本教材的编写参阅了大量的文献,在此谨对各文献作者表示感谢!

本书附有课件,可通过扫描下面或封底的二维码下载,也可从东南大学出版社网站上"读者服务"栏目中下载。

《跨文化交际与礼仪》的编写是一个不断探索、求新求精的过程,在编写过程中,编者力求各方面达到完美,但鉴于编者的知识水平有限,教材中定然有疏漏之处,恳请专家和读者批评指正。

教材编写组
2018 年 11 月

目 录
CONTENTS

Chapter 1	**An Introduction**		1
	1.1	Culture	1
	1.2	Communication	4
	1.3	Intercultural Communication	8
	1.4	Global View on Intercultural Communication	11
Chapter 2	**Philosophies and Values in Different Cultures**		17
	2.1	Introduction	17
	2.2	Major Chinese and Western Philosophical Views	19
	2.3	Different Values in Two Cultures	22
Chapter 3	**Daily Verbal Communication**		33
	3.1	Introduction	33
	3.2	Form of Address	33
	3.3	Initiating Conversation and Conversation Topics	39
	3.4	Greeting, Invitation and Parting	42
	3.5	Gratitude and Apology	47
	3.6	Compliments and Responses	50
	3.7	Visiting and Dining	54
Chapter 4	**Verbal Communication**		60
	4.1	Culture-Loaded Words	60

		4.2	Proverbs	65
		4.3	Taboos	71
Chapter 5	**Nonverbal Communication**			79
		5.1	Introduction	79
		5.2	Time Language	83
		5.3	Spatial Language	85
		5.4	Body Language	88
		5.5	Paralanguage	94
Chapter 6	**Social Customs and Etiquette**			99
		6.1	Introduction	99
		6.2	Traditional Chinese and Western Festivals	100
		6.3	Customs and Ceremonies of Baby's Birth	107
		6.4	Different Birthday Celebrations	110
		6.5	Different Grown-up Ceremony for Children	113
		6.6	Different Rituals of Marriage	115
Chapter 7	**International Business Etiquette**			126
		7.1	Introduction	126
		7.2	General International Business Etiquette	127
		7.3	Some Golden Rules of International Business Etiquette	139
Chapter 8	**Customs and Etiquette of Some Countries**			147
		8.1	Oriental Culture	147
		8.2	Occidental Culture	152
		8.3	Middle-Eastern Culture	159
		8.4	Main African Cultures	165

Supplementary Reading   Social Customs and Etiquette of Some OBOR Countries   172

References   186

Chapter 1   An Introduction

1.1 Culture

1.1.1 Definition

What is culture? There are various definitions.

According to the *Concise Oxford Dictionary*, culture is "the arts and other manifestations of human intellectual achievement regarded collectively". It refers to intellectual perspective, such as music, art, exhibition, dance, etc. When you talk about Mozart, Da Vinci, etc., you are talking about culture.

Anthropologists believe that culture is "the customs, civilizations, and achievements of a particular time or people". In this sense, there are Greek culture, Egyptian culture, Chinese culture, Babylon culture and so on.

Psychologists define culture as "the collective programming of the mind which distinguishes the members of one category of people from another". For example, Western wedding ceremony is different from Chinese wedding ceremony.

From Intercultural Communication Perspective, culture is a learned set of shared interpretations about beliefs, values, and norms, which affect the behavior of a relatively large group of people.

1.1.2 Images of Culture

1) Culture is Like an Iceberg

Like an iceberg, only a small part of culture is visible. Aspects of culture that we can easily observe are often referred to as objective culture, which includes things such as history, literature, and customs. When we learn the facts about our own or other cultures, we are learning the objective culture. Most part of culture is below the surface of our awareness and not easily observable. The invisible part is referred to as subjective culture which includes feelings and attitudes about how things are going and how they should be going. If we only learn objective culture, we are missing the bigger part that is below the surface.

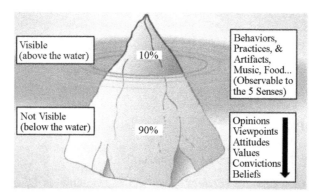

The Cultural Iceberg

2) Culture is Our Software

Geert Hofstede claims that culture is "the software of the mind". As is known, computers do what programs ask them to do. Human beings behave according to their culture. Humans are very similar to computers in this sense. Culture is the basic operating system that makes us human beings. We cannot be said to be human beings until we are programmed by our home culture. At birth the infant is only a potential human and it can be called human until it has learned how to be human in a culturally specific way. It is the culture that provides us with the software. It usually fades into the background and we are only vaguely aware of it as we use it. Sometimes it does not work because it is incompatible with some other software, then culture shock arises.

3) Culture is Like the Water a Fish Swims in

The fish lives and finds food in the water and reproduces and protects itself from danger. It scans everything around it except the water it lives in. The fish takes the water for granted because it is totally used to the surroundings and it really cannot imagine another environment. The same is true for our humankind. Culture is so much about who we are and what the world is like around us, but most of the time we do not notice it and take it for granted.

4) Culture is the Story We Tell Ourselves about Ourselves

Every culture group has a story that provides a way for members of the group to understand who they are and what the world is like. People tell themselves their own stories in their folklore, arts, politics and even intimate conversations among friends and family members. The stories may be very old and include legends of how the group was created, but stories also change to adapt to changing circumstances.

For instance, Chinese often say that China is an old country while the United States is very young. This seems to be true if American culture is assumed to begin with the European settlement of North America or American independence. In fact American culture is an extension of Western culture which can be traced back to the ancient Greeks or even the ancient Egyptians. Someone may argue that American culture is just as old as Chinese culture, but that is not what matters. What is significant is that Chinese tell this story and use it to define who they are as Chinese are in comparison to other groups.

5) Culture are the Rules of Our Behavior

Culture is about how people behave appropriately in their societies. It includes all the rules that make actions meaningful to those acting and to the people around them. Everyone learns to speak by using the grammar of their native language automatically, but they use it with little or no conscious awareness of the rules of grammar. Similarly, people learn their cultural grammar unconsciously and apply its rules automatically. Most people find it difficult to describe the meaning system of their own culture. Just as native speakers of a language are usually unable to speak out the grammatical rules of that language unless they have specifically studied the grammar. Like the grammar of a language, cultural rules are repetitive. They are made up of basic patterns that occur again and again. For instance, an important pattern in Chinese culture is the distinction between inside and outside. This pattern shows up in language, traditional architecture and social relationships.

1.2　Communication

1.2.1　Definition

The word "communication" is used in a variety of ways. Before we use the term any further, we should establish a common understanding of its definition. In this book, communication we discuss is defined as the process of understanding and sharing meaning. Communication is considered as a process because it is an activity, exchange, or a set of behaviors—not an unchanging, static product in which we participate. As David K. Berlo, a well-known communication figure writes:

If we accept the concept of process, we view events and relationships as dynamic, ongoing, ever changing, and continuous. When we label something as a process, we also mean that it does not have a beginning, an end, a fixed sequence of events. It is not static, at rest. It is moving. The ingredients within a process interact; each affects all of the others.

——*The Process of Communication*, David K. Berlo, 1960

Communication is a complicated process. It is variable, active, and dynamic. It starts long before the words begin to flow and can last long after the words stop.

Communication is a process that requires understanding. Your professor asks, "What is the ontogeny of your mysogeny?" You hear the words, but you may not be able to understand or interpret them. An Asian student who has to struggle with English as a second language may have trouble with words that most Americans regard easy to understand. Understanding, or grasping, the meaning of another person's message does not occur unless the two communicators can understand common meanings of words, phrases, and non-verbal codes.

In addition to understanding, communication involves sharing. Consider the popular use of the word sharing. We share a meal, an event, and a sunset. Sharing is a gift that people exchange. We share with others when we talk to them alone or in larger groups. Regardless of the context, communication involves sharing.

What exactly is understood and shared in the communication process? When you use language for expression, meaning is the shared understanding of your feelings. When you use language for pragmatic purposes, meaning is the appropriate response that indicates the message has been understood. For example, you ask for a drink, and the other person gives you one. Meaning is the message you construct in your mind as you interpret the message sent.

1.2.2 Context in Communication

Context is important in all communication. There are also significant differences across the cultures in the ways and the extent to which people communicate through context. The American anthropologist Edward T. Hall has described cultural differences in the use of language and context in communication. He calls communication that occurs mostly through language as low context and communication that occurs in ways other than through language as high context. When he talks about the explicit code he is talking about what we call language codes sent through speech and writing and received through listening and reading.

A high-context (HC) communication or message is one in which most of the information is either in the physical context or internalized in the person, while very little is in the coded, explicit, transmitted part of the message. A low-context (LC) communication is just the opposite: i. e, the mass of information is vested in the explicit code.

Any transaction can be characterized as high, low or middle context. HC transactions feature preprogrammed information that is in the receiver and in the setting, with only minimal information in the transmitted message. LC transactions are the reverse. Most of the information must be in the transmitted message in order to make up for what is missing in the context.

Although no culture exists exclusively at one end of the scale, some are high while others are low, American culture, while not on the bottom, is toward the lower end of the scale. We are still considerably above the German-Swiss, the Germans, and the Scandinavians in the amount of contexting needed in everyday life

——*Beyond Culture*, Doubleday, Edward T. Hall, 1976

In modern urban life many transactions that are high context earlier have become low context. More and more people search and receive information from low context sources such as newspapers, textbooks, lectures, road-maps, announcements and instruction sheets. In more traditional societies people are more dependent on personal or relatively high context sources of information. They get the news from their neighbors and they find their way to an unfamiliar place because someone they know shows them the way. The move from a rural to an urban area is a move from a smaller world to a bigger world. In the bigger world people communicate more frequently with people they do not know. When people do not share context or when they do not have a personal relationship, they do depend more heavily on low context sources of information.

Even though modernization and urbanization are factors that influence the amount of context people use when they communicate, they are not the only factors. Japanese culture, for instance, is a very high context even though it is highly modernized and urbanized. In many social situations Japanese communicators continue to send and receive messages through context that would be sent through language in another equally developed culture. To avoid overgeneralizing, it is wise to consider level of development, national culture and the layers or levels of culture when assessing the communication behavior of any individual or group.

Chinese people tend to be high-context communicators as compared to people from Western cultures, but they are not as high on the context scale as Japanese communicators are. As Hall points out, the use of context in Chinese communication extends even to the language.

1.2.3 Culture and Context

People in all cultures use both relatively high and relatively low-context communication. In one culture a situation may be understood to be high context (the message is in the situation), while in another culture a similar situation is one in which participants send and receive messages through languages.

The difference between high and low-context communication is one of the major sources of confusion, frustration and misunderstanding in cross-cultural communication. When people move from one culture to another, they usually think about how they will deal with the differences in language. They study language codes and engage the assistance of interpreters and translators. They seldom pay attention to the significant cultural differences in the use of context in communication.

Think about the typical experience of a Chinese student going to the United States for study as compared with the typical experience of a student coming from the West to study in China. The Chinese student is likely to be met with lots of information mostly in written form. There will be a handbook for the international students and notices on the wall of the registration office about what to do before and after registration. Also there will be a handbook of dormitory regulations and printed information about how to renew different types of visas or how to change them and so on. The Western students arriving in China will get some information of this type, but much less. In fact, Westerners often complain that they don't find out what the situation really is until after they have arrived.

Westerners appreciate the personal help they receive when they come to China, but they also want low-context information to help them plan, act and adjust to a new situation. High-context communicators need the low-context messages they receive, but without human helpers they experience their new cultural situation as cold and impersonal.

Case 1 A fish in unfamiliar water

A Chinese student, confident in her knowledge of American culture, prepares to give a speech in English appropriate for an international audience for an English speaking contest. In the speech she paraphrases Martin Luther King, Jr. by using the phrase "I have a dream". She is confident that her intended international audience will understand the reference.

She is right. The audience will know that she is quoting Martin Luther King, Jr. but they won't necessarily be impressed. King's speech was given thirty-five years ago and is so widely known that quoting it may be considered too simple, as saying what has already been said too many times. In the last years of the 20th century, it might be more appropriate to talk about visions than about dreams. Better yet, the speaker should invent a new and attractive metaphor to carry her meaning. An image from her home culture might be fresher to her audience than her borrowed phrase.

Comment: To most Americans and many other Westerners, time flies by very quickly. So using an out-of-date metaphor reveals you to be out of date. How much worse if you quote Abraham Lincoln or Thomas Jefferson. If you quote Ernest Hemingway to a literary audience your listeners will either think you are a sexist or that you haven't read anything in fifty years. If you quote him to an audience of young people who have technical rather than literal arts training, they may not know who Hemingway is. Even if they do recognize the name, they probably will never have read anything Hemingway wrote.

In Chinese culture, a writer or speaker shows her learning by quoting famous people from the past. It is not necessary to even say where the quotation comes from. The audience will know and will respect your knowledge. In the United States, people rarely quote famous people from the past unless it is an especially sentimental or patriotic occasion where it is understood that old and familiar images should be remembered. Many people attend such events with an attitude of amused nostalgia(对往事的怀念). It might be fun to hear those old clichés(陈词滥调) again.

Americans like to do something unexpected. An advertising executive may get his audience's attention by quoting the ancient Greek philosopher Plato, while a university professor might cleverly surprise an academic audience by using the famous Nike advertisement when he says "just do it".

1.3 Intercultural Communication

1.3.1 Definition

Intercultural communication refers to communication between people whose cultural perceptions and symbol systems are distinct enough to alter the communication event.

Intercultural communication occurs whenever there is communication between people from different cultural backgrounds, for example, what happens on the Silk Road, Marco Polo's stay in China, Monk Jianzhen's mission to Japan, and Zheng He's seven voyages to the Indian Ocean and the Atlantic Ocean. They tell us that intercultural communication is as old as history. Nevertheless, as a discipline, its history is short.

The term "intercultural communication" typically refers to the study of a particular idea or concept within many cultures. The goal of such investigation is to conduct a series of intercultural analysis in order to compare one culture to another on the attributes of interests. Adler says that positive cross-cultural learning experiences typically:
- involve change and movement from one cultural frame of reference;
- are personally and uniquely important to the individual;
- force the person into some form of self-examination;

- involve severe frustration, anxiety, and personal pain, at least for a while;
- cause the person to deal with relationships and processes related to his or her role as an outsider;
- encourage the person to try new attitudes and behaviors;
- allow the person to compare and contrast constantly.

Intercultural communication as a field of study first emerged in the United States in the 1950s as a result of the four trends that lead to the development of the global village.

1) Convenient Transportation Systems

In the form of transportation and communication systems, new technology has accelerated intercultural contact. Supersonic transports now make it possible for tourists, business executives, or government officials to enjoy breakfast in San Francisco and dinner in Paris.

2) Innovative Communication Systems

Innovative communication systems have also encouraged and facilitated cultural interaction. Communication satellites, sophisticated television transmission equipment, and digital switching networks now allow people throughout the world to share information and ideas instantaneously.

3) Economic Globalization

As we enter the 21st century, the United States is no longer the only dominant economic force in the world. For example, according to Harris and Moran (Samovar & Porter, 2003), there are now more than 37,000 transnational corporations with 207,000 foreign affiliates. This expansion in globalization has resulted in multinational corporations participating in joint ventures, licensing agreements and other international business arrangements.

4) Widespread Migrations

In the United States, people are now redefining and rethinking the meaning of the word "American". It can no longer be used to describe a somewhat homogeneous group of people sharing a European heritage. As Ben J. Wattenberg tells us, the United States has become the first universal nation, a truly multi-cultural society marked by unparalleled diversity. (Samovar & Porter, 2003)

1.3.2 Potential Problems and Barriers

1) Anxiety

It occurs because of not knowing what one is expected to do, and focusing on that feeling and not be totally present in the communication transaction.

Sugawara (1993) surveyed 168 Japanese employees of Japanese companies working in the United States and 135 of their U.S. coworkers. Only 8% of the U.S. coworkers felt impatient with the Japanese coworkers' English. While 19% of the Japanese employees felt their spoken English was poor or very poor, 20% reported feeling nervous when speaking English with U.S. coworkers, 30% of the Japanese employees felt that the U.S. coworkers were impatient with their accent, and almost 60% believed that language was the problem in communicating with the U.S. coworkers. For some Japanese workers, anxiety over speaking English properly contributed to avoiding interactions with the U.S. coworkers and limiting interactions both on and off the job to other Japanese only.

2) Lack of Cultural Sensitivity, Assuming Similarity Instead of Difference

Culture differs from one another and each culture is unique. As we know, culture shapes and influences communication. Two people from different cultures may have difficulty in communication (degree of difference depends on the degree of similarity and dissimilarity between the culture). "You can easily see and accept different hairstyles, clothing, and foods, in basic norms and thinking patterns, however, you may assume that down deep we are really all alike. Actually, we aren't." That is to say, if one lacks of knowledge of intercultural differences, it is difficult to be empathetic. It demands the ability of cultural sensitivity for greater understanding among people from different cultural backgrounds. The TV series *Beijingers in New York* shows that Wang Qiming assumes their friends will take good care of his wife and himself and offer good accommodation when they first come to New York, but on the contrary the friend goes away after welcoming them at the airport and leaves them alone in a totally strange street.

3) Ethnocentrism

Ethnocentrism is a habitual disposition to judge foreign peoples or groups by the standards and practices of one's own culture. Ethnocentric people tend to view alien(外国的) cultures with disfavor and have a sense of inherent superiority. Various forms of ethnocentric attitudes are as follows:

- my culture should be the role model for other cultures;
- I have little respect for the values and customs of other cultures;
- most people would be happier if they live in my culture;
- people in my culture have just about the best lifestyles of anywhere;
- I do not cooperate with people who are different;
- I do not trust people who are different;

- I dislike interacting with people from different cultures.

1.4 Global View on Intercultural Communication

1.4.1 Challenges in a Globalized World

Thirty years ago the Canadian writer Marshall McLuhan introduced the term "global village" to express the idea that the world seems to be getting smaller. The planet Earth is not shrinking, but time and space are. In the metaphor of the global village, nations are like families and continents are like neighborhoods. Residents want to stay on good terms with their neighbors. They may simply think that it is the proper and civilized way to live. They may consider their neighbors to be a lot like them and therefore understand them and like them. They may remember that some neighbors helped them when they had some trouble. Perhaps they have just learned that life is better when people cooperate with one another. If some residents of the village have had trouble with their neighbors in the past or think they are strange or inferior, they may be suspicious and on guard to protect themselves from harm in the future.

As in a village the nations (families) of the world are dependent on one another. Time and space no longer isolate or protect nations and groups from each other. As global environmental problems become more serious, people realize that the rivers of the world flow and the winds of the planet blow without regard to national boundaries. The economic, political and military actions of other nations are the actions of our neighbors. We might wish we could treat them as distant events that do not concern us, but in the global village that is impossible. The residents of the village prefer to see the world in terms of their own family, their own nation. They may say, "We do not want to live in a village that someone else makes for us and controls." They worry that the global economy will force everyone to become like the families of the world that have the most economic and political power. They do not want to be second-class citizens in the village, and they do not want to give up their own treasured ways of life. Whatever anxiety people have about the global village, they can see that contact among the peoples of the world is increasing. If the world is becoming more like a village, as its residents we want it to be a good place to live. Everyone wants to benefit from global trade and advanced technology, and they want to live among people who respect and appreciate one another. They want to protect themselves from danger and live at peace with their neighbors. But most people do not want peace imposed on them by the power of another family. They want to live in their own way.

These are some of the challenges of living in a global village. To meet those challenges people everywhere need to learn about other cultures. They need to know their neighbors. They need to do more than know about them. They need to know how to get along with them and how to solve problems that inevitably arise. To do this it is necessary to learn how to communicate across cultures. That means residents of the global village need to learn to think, feel and behave in new ways. The reality of the global village challenges all its residents to develop a broader worldview, a more global psychology, and the cultural skills necessary for building relationships and solving problems across cultures.

1.4.2 The Importance of Intercultural Communication

It is often thought that people can communicate with foreigners effectively if they have listening, speaking, reading and writing abilities of a foreign language. Actually, it is not the case. Quite often, one polite behavior in a culture may be impolite or even rude in another culture. So it is more important to know "how to say" than "what to say" in intercultural communication. The study of IC will help us in the following three aspects.

1) Taking Objective and Understanding Attitudes Towards Other Cultures

Cultures are different. Through studying IC, we can gain insight into other cultures. It helps broaden our horizon and open our minds to different perspectives and experiences. It helps awaken our cultural sensitivity, the reflection and unlearning of ethnocentrism and help the cultivation of an open attitude and the general development of intercultural personalities.

2) Learning and Inheriting Chinese Culture Better from New Perspectives

Through studying IC, we can compare Chinese culture with other different cultures from all-round dimensions under the background of globalization, and get to know what our traditional culture is, how we can adapt to different cultures. To enrich our national culture we can learn and assimilate all the great cultural achievements of other countries.

3) Making Effective Cross-cultural Communication in a Global Environment

As the result of the formation of "Global Village", today's world is becoming smaller, and people are becoming more closely connected with each other. They are facing the reality of cross-cultural communication in a global environment. They need to deal with international economic relationship, and to solve environmental issues including overfishing,

Chapter 1   An Introduction

global warming, deforestation, endangered species, waste disposal, air and water pollution, and they need to share ideas and information more freely. To achieve these goals, people need to develop their cross-cultural communicative competences.

Exercises

I. **Questions for Discussion**
   1. What is culture in your mind?
   2. Try to list as many cultural groups as you can and tell about the characteristics of those groups.
   3. What cultural puzzles or conflicts have you experienced in intercultural communication and how did you handle them?
   4. What do you think usually leads to misunderstanding in intercultural communication?
   5. Could you please describe the features of high-context communication and low-context communication?

II. **Comprehension Check**

   Decide whether the following statements are true (T) or false (F).

   _____ 1. Culture is a static entity while communication is a dynamic process.
   _____ 2. A term in one language may not have a counterpart in another language.
   _____ 3. Although two cultures may share the same ideas, their meanings and significance may not be the same.
   _____ 4. All people of the same nationality will have the same culture.
   _____ 5. The Chinese way of showing concern is usually appreciated by the Westerners.
   _____ 6. All cultures require and value politeness, but the ways in which politeness is achieved may vary significantly.
   _____ 7. Culture can be seen as shared knowledge, and what people need to know in order to act appropriately in a given culture.
   _____ 8. One's actions are totally independent of his or her culture.
   _____ 9. In intercultural communication, we should separate one's individual character from cultural generalization.
   _____ 10. As the result of the formation of "Global Village", today's world is becoming smaller.

III. Vocabulary

Complete the following sentences with the words given below and each word can be used only once.

| intercultural | collective | empathetic | intellectual | communication |
| shared | learned | perspective | global | dynamic |

1. Without continued learning, the students will lose their _____ vitality.
2. I do feel deeply the strength of the _____.
3. Your anxiety is a _____ reaction, and it is nurtured and sustained by the events of your everyday life.
4. Their friendship developed through their _____ interest in the arts.
5. The process is essentially _____ with ideas and feedback flowing both ways.
6. The author of the novel uses a great deal of _____ artistic methods.
7. Here are some tips to assist you in your _____ communications.
8. It is high time to consider the problem on a _____ scale.
9. Try to see the issue from a different _____.
10. Speech is the fastest method of _____ between people.

IV. Translation

Translate the following Chinese phrases into English and vice versa.

1. 多元文化社会
2. 跨文化差异
3. 民族优越感
4. 跨文化交际能力
5. 适应不同的文化
6. intellectual perspective
7. intercultural communication
8. global village
9. cultural sensitivity
10. national boundaries

V. Case Analysis

Case 1

Two men met on a plane from Tokyo to Hong Kong. Chu Hon-fei was a Hong Kong exporter who was returning from a business trip to Japan. Andrew Richardson was an American buyer on his first business trip to Hong Kong. It was a convenient meeting for

Chapter 1 An Introduction

them because Mr. Chu's company sold some of the products Mr. Richardson has come to Hong Kong to buy. After a bit of conversation they introduced themselves to each other.

Mr. Richardson: By the way, I'm Andrew Richardson. My friends call me Andy. This is my business card.

Mr. Chu: I'm David Chu. Pleased to meet you, Mr. Richardson. This is my card.

Mr. Richardson: No, no. Call me Andy. I think we'll be doing a lot of business together.

Mr. Chu: Yes, I hope so.

Mr. Richardson (reading Mr. Chu's card): Chu, Hon-fei. Hon-fei, I'll give you a call tomorrow as soon as I get settled at my hotel.

Mr Chu (smiling): Yes, I'll expect your call.

When these two men separated, they left each other with very different impressions of the situation. Mr. Richardson was very pleased to have made the acquaintance of Mr. Chu and felt they had gotten off to a very good start. They have established their relationship on a first-name basis and Mr. Chu's smile seemed to indicate that he would be friendly and easy to do business with. Mr. Richardson was very particularly pleased that he has treated Mr. Chu with respect for his Chinese background by calling him Hon-fei rather than using the Western name, David, which seemed to him an unnecessary imposition of Western culture.

In contrast, Mr. Chu felt quite uncomfortable with Mr. Richardson. He felt it would be difficult to work with him, and that Mr. Richardson might be rather insensitive to cultural differences. He was particularly bothered that Mr. Richardson used his given name, Hon-fei, instead of either David or Mr. Chu.

Questions:

(1) How do you account for their different impressions?

(2) Does culture play a role in the communication between these two men?

Case 2

An American woman received a letter from a recently married Japanese friend. The Japanese woman wrote in her letter, "My husband is not very handsome. Your husband is much more handsome than mine." The American woman was very surprised at what her friend wrote.

Questions:

(1) Why do you think the American was surprised?

(2) Why do you think the Japanese woman wrote "My husband is not very handsome"?

VI. Role-Play Activities

1. Your American friends will visit you next Sunday. Your family and you discuss about how to host them in your family. Your discussion will focus on how you can communicate the needs of the low-context culture visitors?

2. You invited your American friends in a big restaurant. You ordered a lot of food that much more than you could have to show your hospitality, but your American friends looked puzzled. Your American friends and you have a conversation. Please role-play this situation.

VII. Video Watching

The Guasha Treatment《刮痧》

Chapter 2 Philosophies and Values in Different Cultures

2.1 Introduction

Miranda, an American girl, is now working in China. She has a Chinese friend, Linda, who is also her colleague, 28 years old. Recently, Miranda noticed that Linda was not as happy as she used to be. After Linda explained to her the cause, Miranda felt rather puzzled. It turns out that Linda's parents have been urging her to get a boyfriend and so she could have her own family soon. But to their disappointment, Linda shows little interest in marriage at present because she enjoys her single life very much. Due to the different attitudes toward marriage, conflicts frequently arise in the family. What puzzles Miranda is that whether or not to get married is a very natural and personal option, which even one's parents should not interfere in. She could not figure out why Linda's parents are so worried about their daughter's personal matter. In her eyes, Linda, should have an full control of her own life as an adult does.

Discussion: can you explain to Miranda why Linda's parents hold such an attitude toward her marriage issue? And try to list some differences between China and the West from the perspective of family relationship.

Chinese culture and the western culture both evolved from their own culture origins or backgrounds, which are constituted by elements from many aspects, such as philosophies, economic systems and geographical conditions etc. The chapter will try to explain the cultural origins from the philosophical perspective.

Chinese culture is usually known as a farming culture system which combines Confucianism and some religious ideologies, such as Buddhism, Daoism etc. Confucianism has exerted huge influence on the formation of the Chinese value system, which works as the foundation of Chinese social order. The major doctrine of Buddhism points out that all the sufferings are aroused by the lust in people. Therefore, learn to resist various temptation and inhibit human beings' desires is the ultimate objective for a person to achieve all the life. Daoism focuses on the way to behave properly in order to improve one's character. It has influenced Chinese culture through its speculative(思辨的) philosophical ideas which helped to form the Chinese antithetical(对立地) thinking pattern, mediocre way of doing things, modest principle in communication and benevolent humanism. These cultural origins worked together over the long history to produce a traditional Chinese culture centering around benevolence, modesty and obedience.

The western culture origin can be traced back to the Hebrew(希伯来) culture, the ancient Greek and Roman culture, the Christian culture, Renaissance humanism and the Enlightenment ideas. The Hebrew culture was first founded in the Arabian area. As a nomadic(游牧) group, the Hebrews brought their culture to the Europe when they moved west and north. The Hebrew culture got to know the world through various senses, which was reflected in its connecting objects with functions and its pursuit of practicality, fairness and morality. Then, though later than the Hebrew culture, the ancient Greek civilization and the Roman civilization appeared and were commonly accepted as the cradle of the western culture. The geographical conditions of the Greece cultivated the character of ancient Greek, a love for nature, imagination, intelligence and strength. They attached much value to this life, independence and individuality. The Ancient Greek literature, philosophy and art all demonstrated their thinking about universe, nature and life. This culture was further developed by the ancient Roman civilization. As time went on to the Medieval age, Christianity gradually became the mainstream religion attracting a large number of followers. The Christianity philosophy dominated the entire western society. Its followers believed in the everlasting existence of God and His omnipotence(无所不能). God was the ultimate truth. For several hundred years, scientific philosophies could find little space for development. However, afterwards, the Renaissance and the Enlightenment ages came and helped science and democracy regain life, which eventually laid the foundation for the modern western value system focusing on freedom, equality, and science.

Chapter 2 Philosophies and Values in Different Cultures

2.2 Major Chinese and Western Philosophical Views

To acquire a better understanding of these cultural origins, it is necessary for us to compare and analyze some major philosophical views and ethical values between Chinese culture and the western culture.

2.2.1 Chinese Philosophy

Philosophy, (from Greek, "love of wisdom"), is the rational, abstract, and methodical consideration of reality as a whole or of fundamental dimensions of human existence and experience. Philosophical inquiry is a central element in the history of many civilizations.

Chinese philosophy focuses on cultivation of human beings. The ultimate objective of is to achieve a harmonious state of "the unity of the body and mind," and "the unity of man and nature". These thoughts are presented clearly in Daoism and Confucianism.

The basic world view of Chinese people is human-oriented, different from those of many other cultures. Atheism(无神论) is the base. A key concept is about the phenomenon of cycle. The idea of cycle stemmed from ancient Chinese's observation of daily life: day and night change alternately, four seasons exchange regularly year after year, and the moon waxes and wanes in cycle. In their eyes, the nature, as a whole, worked in cycle. The image of cycle appeared in the *Book of Changes*(易经). It is, thus, believed that the Chinese philosophical ideas were firstly demonstrated in the *Book of Changes*. Afterwards, the Laozi developed and further interpreted the thoughts in the book. Therefore, both the *Book of Changes* and the Laozi are seen by many historians as the earliest source of Chinese philosophy.

Confucianism, in a sense, was developed from the *Book of Changes*, too. It was adopted as the mainstream philosophical ideology of Chinese society for a rather long period. Its founder, Confucius (also called Kongzi), was a great educator of the Spring and Autumn periods. Confucianism put forward a lot of philosophical ideas on morality, politics, ethics and education, which has influenced the Chinese society profoundly.

Ren(仁) is the core of Confucianism, which means to love people. According to Confucius, Ren represents the highest standard for morality. In education, it refers to the

equal right to receive education. In politics, it requires that the ruler should govern the country by moral tools. To achieve that, *Li*(礼) should be strictly abided by, which means that everyone should follow the fixed and right social order. *Li* and *Ren* are two important strategies in governing. To Confucius, a lasting and stable society can be realized only through morality and ritual education. Therefore, he advocates a ruling of morality(德治) and a ruling of man (人治). A ruling of morality is to influence people, no matter they are good or bad, by moral actions. This is the most fundamental way to cultivate a person. A ruling of man puts more emphasis on human value. Human beings are of ethical(伦理) nature, therefore, ethical education should be stressed in the country and society. For thousands of years, Chinese people live with various ethical values which guide their speech and action in family and in society.

Daoism is regarded as both a philosophical ideology and a religion. Philosophical Daoism traces its origin to ideology of Laozi, an extraordinary thinker during the sixth century B.C. Laozi is said to have written a short book, *Daodejing* (or the *Laozi*) which is translated as the "Classic of the Way and Virtue." With its pervasive influence on Chinese culture, it also affects some

neighboring countries. It is concerned with the Dao(or the Way) and how it is realized through what the text calls "naturalness"(自然) and "nonaction"(无为).

In the early Chinese literature, Dao refers to the right or proper course, and the doctrines or teachings that set forth such a course. Laozi, for example, states, "The great Dao is very even (flat, easy to travel on), but people like (to take) by-ways." Dao is said to be the "beginning" of all things. "Dao gives birth to one; one gives birth to two; two gives birth to three; three gives birth to the ten thousand things". The concept of "nonaction," serves to explain naturalness in practice. Nonaction does not mean total inaction. According to the *Laozi*, many human problems are attributed to excessive desire, or a violation of naturalness. Naturalness encompasses only basic human needs, differnt from a greedy desire which knows no end.

Nonaction, at the personal level, means having few desires. At the political level, according to the *Laozi*, the aggressive measures such as war, cruel punishment, and heavy taxation should be condemned because these only reflect the ruler's own desire for wealth and power. If the ruler could rid himself of excessive desires, the world would be at peace.

Besides, Daoism is full of humanism connotation. For example, it teaches people to try to keep healthy, prolong their life, and become immortals.

To sum up, Chinese philosophies focus on human beings. Confucianism and Daoism are two dominant ideologies in history. After the Opium War, a trend of Western learning (西学) triggered a self-renewing process of Chinese philosophy, which endeavored to integrate the western philosophy with the traditional Chinese philosophy.

2.2.2 Western Philosophy

Originated from the ancient Greek philosophy, Western philosophy went through different stages: ancient Greek philosophy, Christian philosophy, modern philosophy etc. Though different branches have grown from its body since the ancient Greek philosophy period, the philosophical spirit remains unchanged, that is, an attention to the causes behind various phenomena, the pursuit of certainty and the origin of the world, and a logical thinking.

Western philosophy put the universe and its origin at the center of the study. For instance, Thales(泰勒斯), an ancient Greek philosopher, thought that the origin of the universe was water. Another philosopher, Heraclitus(赫拉克利特), believed that fire was the origin. Different philosophers provided different answers for the world origin.

In the history of ancient Greece, there emerged three giants successively: Socrates, Plato and Aristotle. Their achievement in science, philosophy and education exerted enormous influence on human society.

Socrates often quoted "know thyself"(了解自己) to instruct people. His words, deeds and thoughts were recorded by his students including Plato. Socrates loved knowledge and persisted in the pursuit of truth. His wisdom lighted up the students' mind, he was just and upright, and to defend his standpoint, he committed suicide. Socrates insisted on guiding students to think independently and seek answers through enquiry. His method was called art of midwifery(精神助产术).

Plato was the founder of Western objective idealism(客观唯心主义). His philosophy

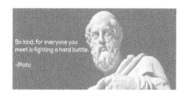
system is extensive and profound, which is mainly reflected in his works, *The Republic*(理想国) and *The Laws*(法律篇). *The Republic* depicts an ideal picture of Utopia(乌托邦). Plato believed that the state should be ruled by philosophers. This ideal country requires everyone to serve a social function to meet the social needs. In this country, women and men enjoy equal rights. In *The Laws*, Plato pointed out that "constitutional state"(宪法国家) was the best state next to the Utopia.

Aristotle, Plato's student, once said, "Plato is dear to me, but dearer still is truth." His persistence in pursuing truth was clearly demonstrated. Aristotle advocated that education should become the function of the state and that schools should be managed by the state. He claimed that the natural quality, habits formation and rational cultivation(理性培育) should be regarded as the three sources of moral education.

One important spirit of ancient Greek culture is in its rational pursuit, which demands a thorough self-reflection(自省) and doubt to reach the ultimate truth. This gave birth to the western science. Another spirit is freedom. Freedom makes people independent. It motivates a respect for individuals and is the basis of democracy.

Christianity dominated medieval culture and all knowledge about the world was based on a complete belief in God. Science was of little value and the respect for speculation(思辨) and rationality was abandoned during that period. At the age of the Renaissance, humanism(人文主义) regained life which activated the spirit of science. Subsequently, the concepts put forward at the Enlightenment(启蒙运动) in the eighteenth century, such as "freedom and equality", "natural rights"(天赋人权) and "social contract"(社会契约) further pushed the development of western civilization.

The western philosophies, originated from the Hebrew culture and the ancient Greek philosophy, over the thousand years, have undergone different periods, including the Christianity time, the Renaissance age, and the Enlightenment, and finally have shaped the modern western society.

2.3　Different Values in Two Cultures

Chen Duxiu, a famous Chinese scholar, once pointed out that Chinese culture was mainly based on family, sentiment and imagination while the Western culture mainly on individual, law and science. Similarly, Hooker said, "The West is rule-based, and China is relationship-based" when comparing the differences between China and the West. In other words, the most significant difference is that: the Western culture relies on an internalized rationality while the Chinese culture lives on self-consciousness.

2.3.1 Values in Chinese Culture

Confucianism is mainly about ethical values which put emphasis on character training and advocate a meaningful life. This chapter lists some specific values that are generally recognized by Chinese people and help people gain an insight into how Chinese culture values work.

1) Collectivism and Family Values

Chinese traditional philosophy stresses "the unity of man and nature" (天人合一), which refers to man's worship and obedience of nature, a harmonious unity with nature. This thinking leads to collectivism and altruism (利他主义). Chinese people tend to pay more attention to collective interests, family or national, inhibit personal desires, and oppose extreme individualism and heroism. They believe: no country, no family; no family, no individual. Personal interests should be properly integrated into collective interests.

Influenced by Confucianism, traditional Chinese family is blood-bonded and ethical-oriented. In the feudal society, there existed a strict hierarchy in Chinese family, which regulated and maintained family relations. Male, father, elder brother occupied the high position in this hierarchy. One core of education is to teach children to show filial piety (孝顺) to parents since they are children. Besides, Chinese people have a strong sense of family. Family exerts huge influence on their life. Marriage is not only a matter of individual, but also a big event of the whole family. In ancient China, one important function of marriage was to fulfil a family obligation, that is, to sustain the stability and continuation of the family. Therefore, it is very common to see that in China, many parents are too concerned with children's marriage.

2) Other Relational Values

Chinese value system is a combination of Confucianism, Daoism and Buddhism. Influenced by collectivism, Chinese people always tend to find their own positions in social relations. Each person plays a different role in a group. Therefore, he/she is usually not conceived as an independent individual, but a kind of relationship involved in the whole society. The following norms can partly reflect the relational orientation values in Chinese ethics, which correlate with each other.

(1) Wu Lun(五伦)

Wu Lun, an essential relational norm in Chinese ethics, means five universal and basic human relationships, which include the relationships between father and son, ruler and subject, husband and wife, elder and younger brothers, and senior and junior friends. Wu Lun contains such regulations as the senior hold mastery of the junior and the junior obey and respect the senior.

These five types of relationship require everybody in the society to find his/her own position and act strictly according to social rules instead of individual willingness.

(2) Authority

Confucianism emphasizes social hierarchy and order. Authorities, teachers, parents, the elders and leaders are trusted and respected by Chinese people. It is regarded as a virtue to be modest, obedient and self-effaced. In Chinese tradition, the accumulation of age is equal to the addition of wisdom and the aged should be respected. Maybe that's why Chinese people tend to enjoy the prestige brought by an increasing age. Hierarchy is honored, and each social member should fulfill his/her duty as defined by the specific social position.

(3) Harmony

In Chinese ethics, a person who has destroyed the harmonious relationship is considered immoral, whether he can be justified or not. Confucianism is often characterized by the moral behaviors in all kinds of relationships to achieve the harmonious social environment: adapting to the group, controlling the emotions, avoiding conflicts and competition. Besides the interpersonal relationship, such harmony orientation also controls the relationship between human beings and the nature. Chinese people treat themselves as a part of nature and believe that human beings should learn how to live in harmony with the nature.

(4) Golden Mean(中庸)

The Doctrine of Golden Mean represents moderation, rectitude, objectivity, sincerity, honesty and propriety. The key principle is that one should never act in excess. For example, traditionally, it would be considered to be quite extreme to solve conflicts among friends through legal process; people usually anticipate others to have more moral self-control or self-regulation in negotiation. This may help explain why the Chinese are always reluctant to resort to the law.

(5) Mianzi(Face) and Renqing(Favor) (面子和人情)

Mianzi and *Renqing* are two typical concepts in Chinese society. Put it roughly, the direct translation of *Mianzi* is "face" in English. It means showing respect to others according to their status and reputation in the society. For the sake of face, Chinese people tend to avoid saying "no" for fear of embarrassment or offending others. They are also very careful not to let others lose face and implicit in expressing disagreement. Being considerate is a morality. The closest translation of *Renqing* could be favor. The favor you once received from others is expected to be returned at a proper time. If you do not return the favor when that moment comes, it could harm the relationship between you and the person who has helped you.

(6) Li(礼)

Confucianism provides a set of guidelines for proper behaviors. Among them, *Li* is an important concept, translated as "etiquette" or "politeness". A person should obey the rules of *Li* so as to live harmoniously with others. The essential function of *Li* is to build the social order upon hierarchical social relationships. *Li* used to function in China as a law.

(7) Yuan(缘)

Yuan is deeply rooted in hearts of Chinese people. It means everything or every relationship happens in a predestinated manner. The predetermination is governed by a powerful external force—supernatural force, which human beings cannot understand or control. With *Yuan*, interpersonal relationships such as friendships or marriages are doomed. *Yuan* may lead to the act of passive fatalism.

2.3.2 Values in Western Culture

1) Individualism and Privacy

In western philosophies, nature and human beings are usually separated, which leads to individualism. Western people emphasize individual interests, pursue human rights and advocate freedom. They believe that if individual interests cannot be guaranteed, collective interests are of little meaning. Westerners worship individualism, personality and self-development. In this culture, modesty, to some degree, indicates a lack of self-confidence. However, it is just self-confidence that equality can help people win respect from others. As is shown in English, there is only one letter that is always capitalized, "I", a strong proof of the importance of self-confidence. In education, clearly, cultivating students' individual interests and abilities is more important than imparting knowledge into them. Students are encouraged to express their thoughts with no fear of offending teachers.

Chinese society is based on family, while western society is mostly on individual. The western nuclear family structure is relatively simple. Parents take the responsibility of raising young children. But once a child gets married, it is natural for he/she move out of parents' home. Parents are not obliged to support their children. It is a sign of independence and freedom. The elders provide the young people with the maximum freedom and cultivate their awareness of living independently. As to marriage, they insist that love should be the basis. Pursuing true love is the most important reason for a marriage. And, it is related to personal choices and has little to do with parents demands.

2) Other Mainstream Ethical Norms

In the highly individualized culture, westerners also share some other ethical norms to regulate their own behaviors.

(1) Norm of Rights and Duties

Rights and duties are inseparable from each other. Rights are based on a set of agreed behaviors and responsibilities. They are given to protect people's basic freedom. Duties are defined as things that are to be completed or be followed by an individual, which represent the moral commitment to someone or something. These two are considered to be two sides of the pillar to establish their society and culture.

It is extremely important for any individual to perform their duties, so as to protect their rights for the benefit of the society.

(2) Norm of Justice

It takes a long time for westerners to discuss on "justice", from Plato's "a state of morality" to Aristotle's "the lawful and the fair", from Augustine's "justice is an eternal standard, which exists prior to the country" to the idea of the classical "Natural La". Freedom, equality, integrity, security and fairness are conceived as the primary values of justice. In the western view, justice combined with the knowledge of laws has a deep root in their life, and it plays an important role in shaping their political and legal system.

(3) Norm of Utilitarianism

Utilitarianism asserts that to do the morally right thing is to maximize the overall amount of happiness. To a utilitarian, the absolute duty is to perform actions which benefit society as a whole. If the only way to increase the happiness of society is to sacrifice one's own happiness, they are morally required to do so. This helps us to understand their commitment to military service: the willingness to sacrifice your own happiness—and even your life—in

Chapter 2 Philosophies and Values in Different Cultures

order to defend the society of which you are a part. In addition, the utilitarian holds the ideal view of respecting others since each individual's happiness is equally important.

2.3.3 Other Differences in Two Cultures

1) Past-oriented vs Future-oriented

Generally speaking, Chinese culture tends to value history and experience, which is past-oriented. For example, we often talk about our long history proudly. We often evaluate a person based on his/her past performance. Some Chinese sayings like "The family has an old, a treasure"(家有一老,如有一宝), "veterans are abler than recruits"(姜还是老的辣), and many expressions such as *laodao*(老道), *Guo Lao*(郭老) etc, all imply a respect for the experienced and the senior. On the contrary, western culture has the inclination of industrial culture, which is future-oriented. It means the potential is more valued than the past. People are not satisfied with what they have achieved. They look forward to the unknown part and are motivated to move on for a better life.

2) Complex vs Simple Interpersonal Relationship

Chinese people's life is filled with various interpersonal relationships due to the strong sense of family. When dealing with relationships, instead of thinking about only one side, Chinese people prefer to think from all sides to avoid hurting the relationship. As a result, a simple matter may often be complicated. Westerners generally deal with their relationships in a relatively simple, straight-forward and matter-of-fact way. They rely more on the rules or laws. Therefore, their interpersonal relationship seems to be less interfered by human factors.

A real story may help us understand the difference. Once when a Chinese was travelling in a western country by car, he was suddenly stopped by a policeman due to an accidental violation of traffic rules. Without much thinking, the driver pleaded with the policeman to forgive his unintentional mistake and let him go without a fine. The policeman listened to him with a smile all the time without any objection. The man misunderstood this as an agreement. So, he drove away happily. It was not until a few months later that he realized he was wrong with the smile when he received a summon from the court. The policeman acted on the law, not giving him a chance to escape the punishment.

3) The Seeking of Stability vs Change

Due to Confucianism, Chinese people think highly of stability. People are eager to strive for social, national and family stability, and to realize the dream of living and working in peace and contentment. They always try to seek development in stability, which in turn helps the culture continue. But this strong belief in stability is also one reason for the conservative character of Chinese people, which, to some degree, has limited the development of individual and society as a whole.

Western culture tends to embrace change, and one of its core ideas is "everything changes", or "change never stops". Innovative ideas are encouraged in the West. Pursuing changes is believed to have a direct relation with its marine culture history. The feature of marine culture is a process of conquering nature and obtaining individual liberation. It welcomes changes and is active in exploring the world, which explains why the western countries developed so fast in the industrial age.

Though many differences on philosophy and value have been listed in this chapter, there still exist some sharing ideas between the two cultures. For example, both appreciate hard work and value of education. Both praise the quality of honesty. It is these sharing ideas that lay the foundation for mutual communication and understanding. With increasing globalization, different cultures correlate with each other. Sometimes, it becomes hard to draw a clear line between different cultures. For example, the young Chinese generation are more aware of privacy and individuality. They are becoming more confident in expressing their opinions. As is clearly shown, cultures keep changing with the time. Studying the origins of the two cultures enables us to analyze the cultural differences from the perspectives of philosophy and value system, which is the basis for cross-cultural communication.

Exercises

I. Questions for Discussion

1. What can be considered to be the origins of a culture?
2. What are the mainstream philosophical ideas in China?
3. Why is the ancient Greek philosophy regarded as the cradle of the western culture?
4. Can you list some different points between the West and China on education?
5. Please compare individualism and collectivism, and try to analyze the features of an individualistic society and a collectivistic society.

Chapter 2　Philosophies and Values in Different Cultures

Ⅱ. **Comprehension Check**

Decide whether the following statements are true(T) or false (F).

_____ 1. Daoism focuses on the way to behave properly in order to improve one's character.

_____ 2. Plato often quoted "know thyself"(了解自己) to instruct people.

_____ 3. Influenced by Confucianism, traditional Chinese family is blood-bonded and ethical-oriented.

_____ 4. The strong belief in stability is also one reason for the conservative character of Chinese people, which, to some degree, has limited the development of individual and society as a whole.

_____ 5. Chinese culture has the inclination of industrial culture, which is future-oriented.

_____ 6. At the age of Renaissance, humanism(人文主义) regained life which activated the spirit of science.

_____ 7. *Ren*(仁) is the core of Daoism, which means to love people.

_____ 8. Philosophy, is the rational, abstract, and methodical consideration of reality as a whole or of fundamental dimensions of human existence and experience.

_____ 9. Traditionally, Chinese people think it would be an extreme behavior to solve conflicts between friends by means of legal process.

_____ 10. According to the *Laozi*, many human problems are traced to excessive desire, or a violation of naturalness.

Ⅲ. **Vocabulary**

Complete the following sentences with the words given below and each word can be used only once.

persisted	obedience	violation	summon	interpersonal
potential	conservative	self-reflection	hierarchy	rationality

1. Socrates loved knowledge and _____ in the pursuit of truth.
2. One important spirit of ancient Greek culture is in its rational pursuit, which demands a thorough _____ and doubt to reach the ultimate truth.
3. In the feudal society, there existed a strict _____ in Chinese family, which regulated and maintained family relations.

4. Chinese traditional philosophy stresses "the unity of man and nature"(天人合一), which refers to man's worship and _____ of nature, a harmonious unity with nature.

5. On the contrary, western culture has the inclination of industrial culture, which is future-oriented. It means the _____ is more valued than the past.

6. It was not until a few months later that he realized he was wrong with the smile when he received a _____ from the court.

7. But this strong belief in stability is also one reason for the _____ character of Chinese people, which, to some degree, has limited the development of individual and society as a whole.

8. Chinese people's life is filled with various _____ relationships due to the strong sense of family.

9. Once in a western country, a Chinese driver was stopped by the police due to his _____ of traffic rules.

10. The most significant differences between the western and Chinese cultures is that: the West relies more on internalized _____ while the Chinese lives on self-consciousness.

Ⅳ. Translation

Translate the following Chinese phrases into English and the English phrases/sentences into Chinese.

1. 《易经》
2. 天人合一
3. 姜还是老的辣
4. 无为
5. 中庸
6. Confucianism
7. rational cultivation
8. interpersonal relationships
9. Plato is dear to me, but dearer still is truth.
10. Influenced by Confucianism, traditional Chinese family is blood-bonded and ethical-oriented.

V. Case Analysis

Case 1

Lin had traveled 20 hours from Beijing to New York. He needed a good meal. His American friend, Mike, met him. But Mike only offered him a plate of roasted chicken and a glass of orange juice. Lin was used to having a main course, and asked Mike if he had any rice. Mike said he only had fried noodles, and Lin had to make do with it. Though Lin knew Americans didn't care very much about what food they ate, he still felt surprised because he had taken Mike to the most famous duck restaurant in Beijing "Quanjude" when he arrived in Beijing.

Question:

Why did Lin feel surprised? Offer some advice to him about adjusting to his new environment in America.

Case 2

I have an American friend. I have invited him several times, and at last he invited me to his home one day. He told me to get there at 3 p.m. I thought we could chat and have a meal together. I gave him a Chinese calendar, a silk scarf and a bottle of Chinese white wine. He only took out a dish of nuts, a plate of bread and a bottle of wine. After two hours' chat, I found there was no hint of a meal and said good-bye to him. He only gave me a box of chocolate as a present for the New Year. After I got home, I found the box already been opened. I was very surprised.

Question:

What surprised me?

VI. Role-play Activities

Role-play the following dialogue and discuss the questions: what values do you think are reflected in this conversation? How do you comment on the approaches adopted by the speakers?

Ms. Smith: You're not meeting your targets this month!

Mr. Zhao: Apologies... We're certainly trying our best!

Ms. Smith: But quotas are quotas! I want you to get the output stats up. By month end!

Mr. Zhao: We'll get our team together to research the situation. Don't worry! No problem!

Ms. Smith: Is it a supply and delivery snag? Seems like your old friend Zhang's production group is not getting their raw materials to you quickly enough for finishing.

Mr. Zhao: Their whole team is under a lot of pressure.

Ms. Smith: Pressure or no pressure, the company has targets to meet. I'll call Zhang up right now and get this squared away.

Mr. Zhao: No need to! It's OK. We can work it out among our groups. We'll take responsibility. Don't worry! No problem!

Ms. Smith: Zhang's responsible and I want this solved now! Let me just ring him, call him in, and get this sorted out.

Mr. Zhao: But...

Ms. Smith: [Putting the call through]

Mr. Zhao: Ohhh... [turning silent, looking at the floor]

Ⅶ. **Video Watching**

1. *Seven* by David Fincher (1995)
2. 《孔子》 胡玫 (2010)

Chapter 3 Daily Verbal Communication

3.1 Introduction

Verbal communication refers to the use of spoken or written words to relay a message. It serves as a vehicle for expressing desires, ideas and concepts and is vital to the processes of learning and teaching.

In daily verbal communication, there are many routine ways people should observe in order to keep smooth cross-cultural interaction. If people are ignorant of cultural differences, intercultural communication tends to fail. With some knowledge of the basic cultural difference, one is likely to survive in other cultures. Different ways in daily verbal communication in Chinese and Western cultures will be discussed in the following parts.

3.2 Form of Address

As an important part in verbal communication, address form is considered as the first message conveyed from speakers to addressees in many situations. Address forms are common phenomena in human verbal communication in daily life across cultures. They make up one of the most important parts of language word systems and reflect the speaker's and addressee's role and identity, family and social status, intimacy or remoteness of their relationship as well as their likes and dislikes.

Addressing is a systematic, variable social phenomenon. Different nations have their own unique addressing systems. Appropriate addressing behavior is crucial for the establishment and maintenance of interpersonal relationships.

1) Personal Pronouns

Personal pronouns refer to the pronouns people use to call each other between the interlocutors. In English and Chinese there's a relative different personal pronoun system. First, Chinese has two forms of the second person pronoun, i.e. "你" and "您", respectively used according to degrees of politeness, whereas English has only one form, i.e. "you", which refers to two persons or more, as well as only one person. Second, considering their frequency of use, personal pronouns are more widely used in English greetings than in Chinese. Take the followings as examples:

(1) How are you doing? / How are you recently?
   怎么样,最近?

(2) Hey, are you OK? / Hey, you good?
   嗨,挺好的吧?

(3) How is your thesis?
   论文写得怎么样了?

(4) How's it going with your business?
   生意都还好吧?

Third, the first person pronoun is also seldom used in Chinese greetings. For instance:

(1) 久闻大名! I have heard a lot about you.

(2) 幸会幸会! I am happy to meet you.

Chinese has evolved a whole set of honorific(敬称) and humble bound forms prefixed to terms of address, one's house and so on, in place of first and second person pronouns. Wang Li (1954) believes that the use in classical Chinese of the first person pronouns "吾" and "我" is considered to be impolite except in conditions of familiarity or intimacy. Thus the ancients had a politeness rule in regard to terms of address, which was to avoid using pronouns as much as possible and substitute names and terms of address for them. This avoidance strategy explains why Chinese has so many different pronouns, like "君"、"公"、"先生"、"阁下"、"陛下"、"足下"、"臣"、"弟子"、"学生" etc., so do Japanese and other Asian languages.

Due to the increasing awareness of equality in everyday life, many of the very formal honorifics have been out of use, but some are still heard in a specialized community sometimes, academic circles, for instance.

2) Personal Names

Although English and Chinese share in common two types of personal names—a surname/ family name/ last name and a given name/ first name, the order of these names is quite different.

In Chinese the surname comes first and is followed by the given name, e. g. Li Aijun (李爱军), while in English the order is totally reversed, e. g., Michael Jordan.

In most English-speaking countries, people's name form is Given Name plus (X) plus Surname. X can be a zero form or can be a middle name. The first name could be one's Christian name or given name, but in many Western countries, parents tend to give their children more than one given name. Thus they have a second structure. Middle name can be one's second given name while one's first name is not a Christian name. In this structure, middle name is not as important as first name (Christian name or first given name), and it is quite common for Westerners to omit or abbreviate the middle names. For example, Robert Delano Roosevelt can be rewritten as Robert D. Roosevelt.

With one-character or two-character given name in China, it is considered as an entirety either in semantic meaning or in pragmatics. For example, when we are introducing someone in China, we say, "This is one of my good friends. Her family name is Zhang(张) and given name is Lili(丽丽)." Lili(丽丽) is an entirety that cannot be parted. Besides, there are at most four characters in one's full name in Chinese. There are a few dissyllabic surnames like Ouyang(欧阳), Situ(司徒), Shangguan(上官) before given names. Under this circumstance, we tend to address a man named "欧阳军" as "欧阳" and one called "司徒浩然" either as "司徒" or "浩然". This is a quite unique phenomenon in Chinese to which there is seldom any equivalent in other languages.

While in English the numbers of one's given names can be optional. For example, the longest name in the world belongs to a man living in Philadelphia, U. S. A. His name is as follows:

Adolph Blaine Charles David Earl Frederick Gerald Hubert Irvin John Kenneth Llyd Martin Nero Oliver Paul Quincy Randolph Sherman Thomas Uncas Victor William Xerxes Yancy Zeus Wolfe-schlegelstein-hausenberger-dorff..., Senior.

3) Popular Address Terms

Popular address terms, also known as "common address terms", refer to terms or phrases that can be applied to any person in a community regardless of professions, posts and ranks, or even ages.

In Chinese, the most preferred popular address terms are "同志"、"师傅"、"老师"、"先生"、"女士"、"小姐", etc. They can be used after the last name or the full name to form compound address terms such as "姚先生"(family name plus Mr., Mr Yao)、"志超同志"(given name plus comrade, Comrade Zhichao)、"姚志超同志"(comrade plus full name, Comrade Yao Zhichao)、"宋女士"(family name plus Lady, Lady Song)、"茹云小姐"(given name plus Miss, Miss Ruyun)、"宋茹云小姐"(full name plus Miss, Miss Song Ruyun), etc.

Among the above-mentioned compound address terms, "姚先生"、"姚志超同志"、"宋女士"and "宋茹云小姐"are applied between strangers or in formal occasions while "志超同志"and "茹云小姐"are used to address acquaintances to show intimacy or personal affinity. Recent development shows a significant rise in the use of "beauty(美女)", "dude(帅哥)" and an overwhelming decline of "同志"and "师傅".

English popular address terms include "Sir", "Madam", "Miss", "Mr.", "Mrs." and "Ms". "Sir" and "Madam" can be addressed alone to show a rather formal and remote relationship. However, the most widely used address form is "Mr. (Mrs., Ms., and Miss) plus family name" such as "Mr. Smith", "Mrs. Johnson" and "Ms. Brown".

4) Relation Address Terms

Relation address terms are terms that are used to indicate social relationship, although in some cases, the relationship between interlocutors can not be identified simply from the address terms. Chinese relation terms include "老师"(student to teacher)、"同学"(student to student/teacher to student)、"师傅"(apprentice to master)、"老板"(employee to employer)、"老大"(subordinate to superordinate)、"老乡"(fellowman to fellowman)、"医生"(patient to doctor), etc. These terms can be applied either directly to the addressees, or together with given name, family name or full name to form compound address terms such as "陈老师"(family name plus term)、"莉莉同学"(given name plus term) and "李军同学"(full name plus term).

However, it should be noted particularly that using relation terms in some cases does not necessarily reflect the real relationship between interlocutors. For example, Chinese students tend to use "老师"to address anyone who works at school, whether they are teachers or not.

In Jinan, the capital city of Shandong province, people usually address any stranger from whom they want to ask for a favor as "老师", usually with an abrupt falling intonation ended with "儿".

Compared with so many relation address terms mentioned in Chinese, the relation terms in English are relatively few, i.e. "Doctor", "Father" and "Boss". "Doctor" is used by the patients to call the doctors; "Father" is used to address the priests; "Boss" is used by employees to address employers only if they are close in relationship. However, "Boss" is seldom addressed directly.

5) Post and Rank Address Terms

Post and rank address terms are very popularly used in a variety of occupational and professional occasions in China. This particular kind of address terms are applied to professions respected and honored by the majority, for example "老师"(teacher)、"医生" (doctor)、"工程师"(engineer)、"经理"(manager)、"教练"(coach)、"记者"(journalist)、 "律师"(lawyer), etc.

Titles can also be used as address terms, including official titles such as "主席" (President)、"书记"(Secretary)、"总理"(Prime Minister), professional terms like "教授" (professor)、"总监"(Chief Inspector), academic titles like "博士"(Doctor), military rank titles such as "将军"(General)、"大校"(Colonel)、"少校"(Major)、"中尉"(Lieutenant) and "中士"(Sergeant), etc. All of the titles can be added with family name.

Particular attention should be paid to official titles, which comprise a great percentage of address terms in official and formal occasions. In addition to examples given above, other commonly used terms are, "部长"(Minister of a Department)、"委员长"(Chief Chairman of a Committee)、"省长"(Governor), etc. There are also "副部长"(Deputy/Acting Minister)、"副主席"(Deputy Chairman/Acting Chairman)、"副主任"(Deputy/Acting Director), etc., indicating slightly lower positions. "Deputy" or "Acting" will be omitted when addressing them by title.

There are also a category of English post and rank address terms, but much fewer compared with Chinese ones.

(1) Professional terms include "Doctor", "Father", "Professor" and "Boss", used without family name;

(2) Official titles are addressed with popular address terms, i.e. "Mr./Mrs./Ms. plus official title" such as "Mr. President", "Mrs. Ambassador", "Ms. Foreign Minister";

(3) Military titles are also addressed with popular address terms, such as "Mr.

Major", "Mr. Colonel", "Mr. Captain", etc;

(4) Academic titles can be addressed with family name. Such as "Dr. Stevenson", "Dr. Smith" and "Dr. Thomas", "Professor Thompson", "Professor Bloomer" and "Professor Wang", etc.

6) Honorific Address Terms

Honorific address terms are terms universally accepted and regarded within a society as a sign of courtesy and politeness.

There are a large vocabulary of honorific address terms in China, coming along with both self-effacing(自谦) terms referring to oneself and appreciatory terms used on others. For example, addressing in the form of "先生"、"同志"、"老"、"公" with either family name, given name, or full name indicates respect for the addressees because of the traditional Chinese value of seniority. The order of the components can be diverse, such as "family name plus Lao" as in "钱老", "full name plus 同志" as in "雷锋同志" etc. The Chinese character "公" can also be used instead of "老" with family name to address people with respect such as "周公"、"夏公".

Besides, a number of popular terms are used especially for honorific purposes, such as "先生"、"老师" and "夫人"(here "夫人" doesn't necessarily means wife, but denotes a lady with a high social status and elegant behavior).

Likewise, the use of "老师" is unnecessarily restricted to teachers, but to anyone who enjoys unanimous respect from the public. For example, the late comedian Ma Sanli(马三立) was the most prestigious traditional "Xiangsheng" (cross talk)—a kind of performing art exclusive to China) master. Though not a teacher, he was revered as "马三立老师" or "马老" by audiences all the time. "先生" is addressed to respectable and learned scholars regardless of gender such as "钱钟书先生" (a famous Chinese scholar)、"杨绛先生" (Qian Zhongshu's wife). In comparison, "太太" or "夫人" indicates an upper social status. Therefore when addressed as "夫人" the woman must come from a prominent family, particularly in terms of politics.

Common English honorific terms are "Sir", "Lady", "Madam" and "Lord", etc. "Sir" can either be used alone or with given name, such as "Sir William", indicating seniority and high social status. "Lady" is addressed to females to show respect; "Lord" is used to refer to aristocrats with the form "Lord plus given name" such as "Lord Henry". The term "Lady" is normally employed to address the wife of a "Lord", such as "Lady Henry" but not "Lady Gaga" (stage name for a very popular American pop singer currently). While such address terms come across, discretion is demanded.

7) Kinship Terms

Kinship terms are terms for blood relations and affinities. They are used within family community between different members of a family with direct or distant relationship, such as "father, mother, sister, brother, uncle, aunt" in English, "父亲、伯伯、舅舅、姑妈、表哥" in Chinese. But against different cultural backgrounds, each language has its unique kinship system, some are simple, such as in English, the kinship terms only reach three generations. In Chinese tradition, the kinship terms are divided into four groups: paternal group, maternal group, wife's line and affinal group. It is so complicated that no other language can match it.

However, there are a large amount of fictive kinship terms in Chinese. There are estimated sixteen basic fictive kinship terms in contemporary Chinese language. Fictive kinship term is the kinship term used in a social interaction as a social address to address non-family members to show familiarity. It is also known as the generalization of kinship terms with Chinese characteristics. In Chinese people's eyes, society is only a magnified family. Using fictive kinship term can shorten the psychological distance of the speakers, make each other feel esteemed and friendly and result in good communication effect. For example, when you ask a stranger the way, you will appropriately address him or her according to both gender and age. In daily life, people often use kinship terms to refer to neighbors, the family members of the friends and colleagues.

In comparison, no fictive kinship address term exists in English-speaking countries, where kinship terms are rarely addressed to non-relatives but for a few exceptions. For instance, Christians may address each other as "Sisters" or "Brothers" as long as religion is concerned; children may call their parents' friends "Aunt" or "Uncle" if they are close, but such terms are only applicable to children.

3.3 Initiating Conversation and Conversation Topics

"Western ideas of privacy are different from those of Chinese." Beal pointed out in a letter to *China Daily* (Dec. 5, 1984). Both Beal and Farebrother (letter to *China Daily*, Oct.

23,1984) pointed out that Chinese often irritate Westerners by the way in which they try to start conversations. The problems often lie in:

(1) the predictability of the questions

Where are you from? /Are you from America?
How can I improve my English?

(2) the invasion of one's privacy

How old are you?
Are you married? /Where is your husband or wife?
How much do you earn?

(3) little attention paid to the answers already given

Conversations between strangers normally occur in natural, not contrived (arranged in a way that seems false and not natural) circumstances. There are many topics that are acceptable to both Westerners and Chinese, such as:

Hobbies
A local or national event
Holidays
Jobs
The weather
Films/books

However, there are some topics that many Westerners regard as private matters, which should be carefully talked about.

1) Age

As is well known, it is impolite in Western culture to ask a person about his or her age. This is particularly true of a woman who is over thirty. Therefore a direct question like "How old are you?" should be avoided.

There is a risk here because we can't sometimes judge others' age, especially for the Asians who generally look younger than their age.

2) Money

Income is deemed as a quite personal and private issue in the West. Even within families, people often do not know the exact salary of other family members. This does not mean that the family members are not close to each other. Therefore in daily communication it is advisable to avoid questions like "How much do you earn?".

In contrast, it is very common in China to ask someone about how much they have paid for a particular item. In the West, although people may discuss prices in general, it is not normally acceptable to ask someone directly how much they have paid for something. The issue can only be approached indirectly. The following offers us an alternative:

Chen Bin: That's a nice china! Where did you buy it?
Eric: At the china shop on Jiefang Road.
Chen Bin: Oh. I'd love to buy one myself. Was it very expensive?
Eric: Not really. Actually, I thought it was quite reasonable. I paid fifty yuan for it.

3) Health

When someone feels sick, such as having a cold, fever or cough, it is common to hear the following expressions in China:

Drink plenty of water.
Put on more clothes.

These pieces of advice are in fact just expressions of concern. Westerners often feel offended at being told such things. Phrases like "Put on more clothes" have protective parental overtones, and hence may sound inappropriate to independent Westerners. The concern is normally shown in English by phrases such as:

I hope you'll be feeling better soon.
Look after/ Take care of yourself.
Have you been to the doctor?
Try and get some rest.

4) Family

It is unwise for Chinese to assume that everyone over 25 or 30 is married and has children. Some Westerners never marry at all. Others marry late, and some marry with no children. Questions like "Is your husband/wife with you?" or "How many children do you have?" can make unmarried people embarrassed. This embarrassment can be even worse if people respond "I'm sorry" on hearing that the person is not married.

A general question like "Do you have a large family?" or "Are there many in your family?" will be more appropriate if talking about parents, brothers and sisters, spouse or children.

3.4 Greeting, Invitation and Parting

3.4.1 Greeting

As an essential part of daily verbal communication, greeting is common in both English and Chinese. Rather than to transfer information, the purpose of the greeting is to establish or maintain social contact. In English, the following sentences are common greetings:

Formal greetings:

—(Good) morning/afternoon/evening.
—How are you?
—How are things going?
—How are you getting on?
—How are things with you?

Informal greetings:

—How are things?
—How's everything?
—How's life?
—Hello.
—Hey there.
—Hi.

While in Chinese, formulaic expressions for greeting are the following:

——吃过了吗? (Have you had your meal?)
——上哪去? (Where are you going?)
——去哪啦? (Where have you been?)
——散步去啊? (Are you going for walking?)
——下班啦? (Have you come off work?)

It is obvious that Chinese and English is quite different in the forms of greeting. But pragmatically speaking, they perform similar functions. Therefore, it is no wonder foreigners may feel confused or even offended if they are unaware of this cultural difference. The natural reaction of most English-speaking people to these Chinese greetings would be: "It's none of your business!" or "Are you going to invite me to dinner?"

3.4.2 Invitation

1) Formal and Informal Invitation

Formal invitation is always in written form in both China and English countries, and responding to them is also done in writing in many Western countries. R.S.V.P. (words taken from French "Répondez s'il vous plait" meaning "please reply") is always on the invitation, requesting the invited guest to respond and determine if they will attend or decline the invitation.

A formal invitation is sent for any type of formal affair, including a formal dinner, charity ball, formal wedding, business or social formal celebration.

Informal invitation can either be written or verbal. Informal invitation is used to invite guests to less formal events. They usually include occasions celebrated by family and friends, and more casual business events.

Response to a written informal invitation may be in writing, or it may be verbal depending on the circumstance and the R.S.V.P. request. Sometimes an R.S.V.P. will give a telephone number to call for responding. And there may be an "R.S.V.P. regrets only", which means you only respond if you are not going to be attending.

A verbal invitation, which is always an informal invitation, is responded to verbally. Many times this may occur in the same conversation if the invited guest knows immediately whether or not he or she will be attending. If the person being invited needs to determine if she or he will be available to attend, a verbal response will follow.

2) Different Invitation Expectation

Expectation about when spouses should be included in invitation differs between China and the West.

In the West, both the husband and wife will usually be included in social invitation for dinner in the evening. While in China, it's quite common for only the husband or wife to be invited to a meal with colleagues or friends.

There are business-related social functions that will only include one's colleagues and/or clients, and not spouses, even to an evening dinner in the West.

3) Differences in Declining an Invitation

People in the West don't like to give detailed explanations why they're declining an invitation. Their explanations are usually short and simple, such as "I'm sorry, I can't get away" or "I'm tied up the whole week" or "I'm already busy that night".

While in China, people will give a more detailed explanation to make sure that the person doing the inviting will understand that there is something really important that has to be done, or a prior engagement has already been made. The purpose is to avoid embarrassment to make sure no misunderstanding will occur. Thus, the Chinese detailed explanation sounds unnecessary to Westerners, and the Westerners' short or no explanation sounds impolite to the Chinese.

What's more, to be polite, Chinese sometimes will even pretend to want to come and promise to try to come by saying "我尽量来（I'll try my best to come）." However, a misunderstanding will occur in the intercultural communication. To a Westerner, saying "try my best" means the person may or may not come but will sincerely try. To the Chinese it doesn't sound sincere, but hypocritical(虚伪的).

4) Genuine and False Invitation

When a Chinese says "Let's get together soon!" "We haven't seen each other for a long period. You ought to come around for a dinner." "It's good seeing you. I will invite you to tea later", he usually doesn't take these invitations seriously.

Likewise, Westerners might also say something which sounds like an invitation but never results in actual get-together. This is called "false invitation", in which statements are just expressions of goodwill. Yet they do have social functions in daily communication in that they are indicative of the speaker's positive attitude towards the other party. Take the following for example:

Lily: It is nice talking to you, but I have to go right now.
Peter: OK, perhaps we can meet sometime soon.
Lily: That sounds good. Why not drop in sometime?
Peter: Great. See you later.

The dialogue above might hardly result in an appointment as it is nothing more than a polite expression. The hearer usually doesn't take it seriously either and the proper response would simply be "all right, I'd love to". If the questions about "when" and "where" are raised, the speaker will be quite embarrassed. Let's make a comparison by another example:

Lily: You are moving to Chicago next month? Shall we have a family get-together for a dinner?

Peter: Yeah. So nice of you. we'd love to.

Lily: What about 6 pm this Saturday at my home?

Peter: OK. See you then.

In this dialogue a genuine invitation is extended because Lily has a definite plan in which the specific time and place has been offered.

5) Common Phrases Used for Verbal Invitation

Can you come over and join us?

I'd very much like you to come to our dinner party.

Shall we have a drink at this restaurant?

We'll be glad to have you attend our meeting.

We're having a dance on Sunday. I hope you'll make it.

We're having a party this weekend. Will you join us?

Come and see me next Friday.

I'm meeting my wife after work. Join us.

Why don't you come to the lake with us?

You must join us for lunch.

How about having a drink with me this afternoon?

Do join me for a coffee.

Perhaps you'd care to come to a party on Saturday.

We'd be delighted if you could spend an evening with us.

We'd be so pleased if you could come.

Would you honor us with a visit?

Betty and I are throwing a dinner party this weekend, we'd like you to come.

We were wondering if you and Mary would like to come to have dinner with us.

If you could manage, we'd like you to attend our speech contest on Thursday morning.

6) Common Phrases Used for Accepting a Verbal Invitation

Yes, I will come. Thank you.

I'd very much like to attend. Thank you.

I'd like nothing better.

I'd like to. It would be very nice to attend your party.

I'll be a little late, is that OK?

Thank you. I'd love to!

That sounds like a very nice idea.

I'd love to join you for lunch.

Yes, I'll come. I'm looking forward to it.

Ok. / Lovely. / Rather!

I'd love to!

Well, good for you! Yes, I'll come.

What a delightful idea. Thank you.

That's really very kind of you.

We'd be delighted to accept your invitation.

It would give us great pleasure to spend Christmas with you.

7) Common Phrases Used for Declining a Verbal Invitation

No, I don't think I can.

Sorry I can't. But thanks anyway.

No, I won't be able to.

That's very kind of you to ask, but unfortunately I already have a commitment then, so I won't be able to come.

Much as I'd like to, I'm afraid I won't be free next Sunday.

What a pity, I'm afraid I already have something planned.

3.4.3 Parting

Parting can be a difficult task in any culture. In Western culture, it is common for the guest to indulge in a couple of minutes' small talk while planning to leave, e.g. "Well, it's been lovely to see you, but I must be going soon. I hope we'll be able to get together again before long..." or "Thank you for a lovely evening. I must not hold you any longer." The host will see the guest to the door and say something like "Thank you for coming.".

In contrast, Chinese visitors often stand up suddenly and say, "I'm leaving now", which seems quite abrupt to the Westerners. Unless the host strongly insists he or she stay longer, the guest will move to the door and say "请留步"、"不要送了"、"回去吧"、"再见". For an important guest, the Chinese host will see him or her to the building gate, or even to the bus stop and say something like "请慢走"、"请走好"、"不远送了"、"有空再来". Sometimes they will not go back until the guest is out of sight.

3.5 Gratitude and Apology

3.5.1 Gratitude

Chinese and Westerners have unique forms, vocabulary, scope and process in expressing their thanks. In Western countries, people are generous with their thanks, no matter whether the favor they get is significant or not, such as being offered a seat, receiving a reply to questions and so on. As a matter of fact, they express gratitude on many occasions. Quite different from Chinese custom, Westerners are not only grateful to their superiors, colleagues and strangers, but also to one's friends, relatives, and family members. Gratitude is ubiquitous between parents and children.

However, "thank you" is rarely spoken between relatives, friends, parents and children in China, because Chinese people value collectivism, so they tend to integrate self into a group or community in which gratitude is unnecessary. Chinese people think gratitude between intimate people will make both parties feel shy and may cause estrangement(疏远) and psychological distance between each other.

In daily verbal communication, the following is used to show one's gratitude to others:

Thanks.
Many thanks.
Thanks a lot.
Thank you very much.
Thank you very much indeed.
I really do not know how to thank you enough.

From the first to the last sentence above, the degree of gratitude increases, and the speaker can use any of them to express gratitude. Westerners, in the light of individualism, tend to express gratitude to others, be they strangers or subordinates, family members or friends, for their help. The following is a case in point.

(A staff invites his manager)

Staff: Mr. Brown, would you like to come to dinner next Friday evening? I want to thank you for your help.

Manager: Oh, thanks. I'd like to very much.

In this case, when the staff wants to thank the manager for his help, the manager will say "Thank you". The staff follows the tact principle in the invitation. The sentence type used is "Would you like to..." to express his tactful courtesy and respect for the manager. At the same time when the manager receives the invitation, his response should also be given directly. It can be seen from this example that Westerners are not shy or embarrassed to say "thank you".

3.5.2 Apology

Wherever people are from, East or West, they usually apologize when they do something wrong. Yet the areas and frequencies for the use of apology are different.

1) Areas and Frequency for the Use of Apology

Comparatively, Western people make more apologies than Chinese people do. They will apologize whenever they think they may invade others' privacy.

They pay less attention to power or rank distinction. They may apologize both to people with less power and close relationship. Therefore it is not unusual to hear elder generations apologize to younger generations, or a superior to an inferior.

Even if the trouble is not so serious at all, they will apologize, for example, they may apologize if they cough or sneeze by saying "Excuse me".

2) English and Chinese Expressions of Apology

Excuse me.

I'm sorry.

Sorry about that.

I'm very/so/terribly/awfully/extremely sorry for that.

I can't tell you how sorry I am.

I beg your pardon(for...).

Pardon me.

A thousand pardons for...

Please forgive me(for...).

I apologize.

I must apologize for my rudeness/fault/mistake, etc.

I must beg to apologize for...

I must make an apology for...

May I offer you my profoundest apologies?

May I offer you my sincerest apologies for the wrongs I've done to you.

对不起。

不好意思。

请原谅/谅解（我的过失/鲁莽/错误/粗心）！

我道歉。

难以表达内心的抱歉。

向你表达/致以深深的歉意。

为我的过失/鲁莽/错误/粗心表示最真诚的歉意！

3) Formulaic Responses to Apologies

It doesn't matter at all.

Never mind (about that).

No harm done.

No problem.

Forget it.

Please don't worry.

That's quite all right.

I quite understand.

It's not your fault.

It's nothing.

There is no reason to apologize.

It's really not necessary.

没关系。

不要紧。

没事。

我理解。

不是你的过错。

不用道歉/自责。

What is worthy mentioning is that the Chinese expression "没关系" or "不要紧" could be a response to both gratitude and apology in Chinese. However, they could not be translated into "It doesn't matter" or "Never mind" which are considered the responses only to apology in English.

3.6 Compliments and Responses

Compliment, "expression of praise, admiration, approval, etc" is a kind of human communication. Compliments and praises, part of daily verbal communication, are of great social function because they help establish good relationship and contribute to the smooth process of communication.

3.6.1 Social Function of Compliment

Chinese and English share similarities in the social function of compliment as follows: creating or reinforcing solidarity (loyalty and general agreement between all the people in a group, or between different groups because they all have a shared aim), greeting people, expressing thanks or congratulations, encouraging people, softening criticism, starting a conversation, or even overcoming embarrassment.

1) To Create or Reinforce Solidarity

- —You look fine today, isn't it?

  —Thank you!

  ——李教授,您的书法真不错!

  ——献丑了!

2) To Greet People

- —Well, don't you look cute today? You have such nice clothes.

  —Thank you. I have had this for a while.

  ——丽姐,多年不见,你还是那样年轻漂亮,一点都没变样!

  ——哪里,老了老了,不能和你比了。

3) To Express Thanks or Congratulations

- —Mary, thank you for the gift. It's beautiful.

  —It's my pleasure.

  —You have done a good job! Congratulations!

  —Thank you very much.

  ——王涛,你太厉害了,这次竞赛获得一等奖!

  ——嗨,瞎猫碰到死耗子了!

Chapter 3　Daily Verbal Communication

——陈师傅,您的技术真不错,这么短的时间就把我的电脑修好了!

——没什么,小毛病而已。

4) To Encourage

- —Grandma, the dish is delicious, your cooking is as good as before.

  —Thank you, I am glad to hear that.

  ——同学们,这次考试成绩不错,80%的同学达到了优秀和良好的标准。我相信大家会继续努力,百尺竿头,更进一步。

5) To Soften Criticism

- —You have done a good job in today's speech, but if you pay attention to the eye contact with the audience, your speech will be perfect.

  —Thank you very much, I will take care of that next time.

  ——您文思敏捷,文章流畅,如果再有一手好字,那就锦上添花了。

6) To Start a Conversation

- —The watch you wear looks very nice. Where did you buy?

  —Really? Oh, I bought it when I went to Switzerland last year.

  ——主任,您的头发做得很漂亮啊。

  ——是吗? 我都担心太夸张了呢。

7) To Overcome Embarrassment

- —What a magnificent wedding! The bride looks very pretty, and the bridegroom looks handsome too!

  —Yes, it is the most unforgettable wedding I have attended!

  ——请问您从事什么工作啊? (初次见面)

  ——医生。

  ——真的很不错啊。现在医生的社会地位很高。

  ——哪里啊。一般吧。

It is obvious that in different situations the response to compliment may vary greatly. At an informal level among intimate friends, the reaction tends to be formulaic or even uniform in both English and Chinese. However, these conventional formulas differ between cultures. These groups of most commonly used responses show that native English speakers tend to accept the compliments, at least in form, whereas the Chinese tend to efface (to behave in a quiet way that does not make people notice or look at you) themselves in words, although they do feel comfortable about the compliments.

3.6.2 The Differences of Compliment between Chinese and English

1) Topics

In both Chinese and Western cultures, females are often complimented by their appearance or their hair-dos, while males are often complimented by their abilities or their accomplishments.

In China, the personal cultivation and noble thoughts are viewed as a kind of virtue and it is common for Chinese people to compliment others for their noble characteristics. They think that the inner beauty is the genuine beauty rather than the appearance. While in Western cultures, people compliment others largely on the basis of the outcomes.

2) Target

In Western cultures, it is some kind of social politeness to praise a friend's wife while it is somewhat a taboo in China. Besides, Compliments in China are mostly given to people of higher status, and it is common for a staff to compliment his manager, while in Western countries the interaction is bidirectional(双向的).

3) Personal Pronoun

In English, the first person pronoun is widely used as a subject in compliments. For example:

——I think your coat suits you very much.

——I like your hairstyle.

Chinese complimenting sentences begin with the second person pronoun.

——你的房子真不错!

——你丈夫真有福气!

——我妈说你做饭好吃,果然如她所说啊。

4) Semantic Formula

According to Manes and Wolfson (1981), the overwhelming majority of English compliments contain one of a highly restricted set of adjectives and verbs.

This was a great meal.

You look so nice today.

You did a good job.

I like your haircut.

I love your glasses.

I really enjoyed your class.

Of all the compliments, according to their data, 80 percent are the adjectives and only 16 percent are verbs.

In Chinese, however, positive words expressing compliments are mainly adjectives, adverbs and verbs. For example:

裙子很漂亮。Your/This skirt is very pretty.

这房间真不错。This room is really good.

你真是位经验丰富的老师。You are really an experienced teacher.

你干得不错。You did the job very well.

你很用功,进步也很快。You study hard and make progress very rapidly.

你待人真好。You treat people sincerely.

我特别喜欢你衬衫的颜色。I especially like the color of your blouse.

你该受表扬。You deserve being praised.

5) Syntactic Formula

According to Manes & Wolfson (1981), compliments in American English can be classified into 9 categories. (NP = noun phrase, ADJ = adjective, PRO = pronoun, V = verb, ADV = adverb)

Your blouse is/looks (really) beautiful. [NP is/looks (really) ADJ]

I (really) like/love your car. [I (really) like/love NP]

That's a (really) nice wall hanging. [PRO is (really) a ADJ NP]

You did a (really) good job. [You V a (really) ADV NP]

You really handled that situation well. [You V (NP) (really) ADV]

You have such beautiful hair! [You have (a) ADJ NP!]

What a lovely baby you have! [What (a) ADJ NP!]

Nice game! [ADJ NP!]

Isn't your ring beautiful! [Isn't NP ADJ!]

3.7 Visiting and Dining

3.7.1 Visiting

There are some cultural differences in visiting. Verbal language should be taken good care of when requesting for a visiting. Usually Chinese make statement or command when they mean to make a request for visiting. For example, Chinese may make a Western friend feel uncomfortable by saying "I'm coming to see you this weekend". In fact, what he really means is "Can I come and see you this weekend?" However in the Westerners' eyes, his wording carries the implication "You must stay at home this weekend because I'm coming to see you". This kind of problem arises from different ways of making request in the two languages. The following are some suitable expressions:

(1) I haven't seen you for a long time. I was wondering whether I could come around to visit you sometime.

(2) I'd like to come and see you sometime. Would you be free one afternoon next week?

(3) I would like to come and visit you. Would it be convenient for me to come Wednesday evening?

Westerners are used to organizing and arranging their time in advance, therefore if a Chinese wish to invite them to something important, it is helpful to give them advance notice (at least a week in advance). Otherwise, they may feel offended and refuse to attend.

In the West, if people go to visit someone, they are almost immediately asked if they would like to take off their coat. If they do not take off what is obviously out-door clothing, it is assumed that they are only going to stay for just a few minutes. After taking off their coat, they will be asked to sit down, and then the host may offer something to drink such as tea or coffee. The offer is normally phrased as a question, such as "Would you like a cup of tea?" The guest is expected to answer honestly, and if they say no, the host will not give them any. If they accept, they will be given a cup and expected to drink it all. After finishing it, the host may offer them a second one.

When Chinese visit foreigners, misunderstanding may occur. When the host offers a cup of tea, the Chinese may refuse out of politeness and want the host to offer more times before accepting. If the host does not make more offers, the Chinese may think he is not so hospitable. On the other hand, if they accept the offer but don't drink it at all, this behavior may offend the host. For instance, a girl visited a foreign teacher. She declined the offer of some drink. Later she grew very thirsty but was too shy to ask for a drink.

When Chinese entertain visitors, they are often extremely hospitable on offering food, even if it is not meal time. If guests are invited for a meal, Chinese usually prepare a large quantity of dishes, usually far more than that can be eaten at the time. Conversely, Westerners tend to relate the meal more accurately to the people's appetite and both the quantity and the variety of the meal are far less than that in China.

The Chinese host usually puts the best dish or food on the visitor's plate, which is an expression of hospitality. The visitor's refusal is usually ignored, for in Chinese culture "no" can often be a polite form of "yes". Westerners, on the other hand, usually leave the guest to help himself/herself and do not keep urging him/her to eat more. In China it is acceptable to leave unwanted food on the plate, whereas according to Western custom, it is impolite to do so.

As a result, misunderstanding occurs. If the Chinese are invited to a dinner by a Westerner, they may feel the Westerner is ungenerous because of the small amount of food and also because they are not constantly encouraged to eat more. They may remain hungry after dinner since the food is even not offered a second time after their polite decline. Whereas the Western visitors in a Chinese home often have a pile of food on their plate (including food they do not particularly want), which according to their culture they should finish. But the more they eat, the more they are given.

3.7.2 Dining

1) Different Traditions for Meals

In the West, generally there's only one main course plus two other side dishes, a salad and vegetable, followed by a dessert, rather than many dishes for a dinner. Food proportion is usually prepared and served with proper amount for the guests to eat, without having some left.

Before preparing meals, the hosts may ask guests about any special food requirements to avoid serving a dish that can't be eaten by someone who is a vegetarian or has a diet restriction for health reasons.

The alternative that will sometimes occur is a hostess will prepare an entree with two or three choices so that all guests' needs will be accommodated. An example would be an Italian pasta dinner with one dish containing meat, and another without. The guests then can choose between the two, or take some of each.

2) Different Dining Out Habits

(1) Dining Out in the West

In America and England, when dining out with friends, it's quite common for friends to share the cost of the meal equally among them, to go Dutch, or split the bill, which implies equality between friends. They seldom fight over paying the bill, or grabbing the bill. To a Chinese person this may seem to suggest that he is too poor to pay for the meal. However this behavior is not at all indicative of a person's financial status and ability to pay for the meal. On other occasions, however, Westerners will treat a friend to a meal normally without the expectation that the guest will return the favor by inviting the host to a meal later in China.

When meeting at a pub for drinks, a popular pastime in England, each person in the group will take turns buying a round, asking everyone what they would like and then going to the bar to get the drinks. Those who don't buy a round when it's their turn are frowned upon. This same tradition also occurs in bars in America.

(2) Dining Out in China

In China when dining out with friends, the one who invites others should pay for the meal. If nobody acts as the host, at the end of the meal, everyone may fight over paying the bill, because only paying for oneself might be regarded as mean, miserly or selfish.

Exercises

Ⅰ. **Questions for Discussion**

1. Discuss the differences in addressing people between English and Chinese cultures.
2. What topics are appropriate in initiating a conversation with Westerners?
3. Discuss the differences between English and Chinese compliments and compliment responses.
4. Can you list some social functions of compliments?

5. In Chinese culture, it is common to address people position-linked or occupation-linked, such as "王经理"、"马局长"、"张主任", etc. Do Americans have similar customs?

Ⅱ. Comprehension Check

Decide whether the following statements are true (T) or false (F).

_____ 1. We can address Eric Smith, who is a teacher, as Teacher Smith.

_____ 2. Chinese hospitality toward the Westerners is always greatly appreciated.

_____ 3. "Thank you for coming!" is a typical expression used by Western hosts when the guests just arrived.

_____ 4. Adjectives and verbs are often used to convey compliment message in English, while adjectives, adverbs and verbs are often used in Chinese.

_____ 5. Compliments on others belongings are sometimes an indirect way of request in American culture.

_____ 6. Chinese people give more compliments in daily life than Americans.

_____ 7. Americans tend to be self-effacing in their compliment responses.

_____ 8. Don't take offence—getting the form of address "wrong" is rarely intended to be offensive.

_____ 9. All cultures require and value politeness, but the ways in which politeness is achieved may vary significantly.

_____ 10. Sometimes the Chinese way of showing modesty may be considered as fishing for compliments.

Ⅲ. Vocabulary

Complete the following sentences with the words given below and each word can be used only once.

| address | disgust | token | beckon | elicit |
| mistrust | compliment | efface | abrupt | verbal |

1. He showed his _____ for the movie by leaving in the middle.
2. She showed her _____ of doctors by ignoring her physician's advice.
3. This distant land of deep spirituality, legendary art, architecture, and dramatic scenery _____ the explorer.
4. Boys learn to use language to preserve independence and negotiate their status, trying to hold center stage, challenging and resisting challenges, displaying

knowledge and _____ skill.

5. Shirley did her best to _____ herself at parties.

6. They _____ me on the way I looked each time they saw me.

7. The judge should be _____ as "Your Honor".

8. Rosie's idyllic world came to an _____ end when her parents' marriage broke up.

9. Her tears _____ great sympathy from her audience.

10. Please accept this small gift as a _____ of our gratitude.

IV. Translation

Translate the Chinese phrases into English and vice versa.

1. 恭敬不如从命。

2. 百闻不如一见。

3. 来而不往非礼也。

4. 有朋自远方来,不亦乐乎。

5. 送君千里,终须一别。

6. A miss is as good as a mile.

7. A leopard cannot change its spots.

8. A bird in the hand is worth two in the bush.

9. No discord, no concord.

10. A great debt of gratitude.

V. Case Analysis

Case 1

A British tourist is visiting a Chinese family. The Chinese hostess, Cai Hong, introduces her husband to the guest:

Chinese hostess: Welcome to my home. And this is my husband.

British tourist: Thank you. It's a pleasure to meet you, Mr. Cai. I'm Lucy Taylor.

Chinese host: Have a seat, Madam Lucy.

Question:

Are there any addressing mistakes in this case?

Case 2

On a party, a Chinese showed a photo of his wife to some American visitors. Out of courtesy, they all said: "How beautiful she is!" Also out of politeness, the man replied with what he would have done in Chinese under this circumstance, "Where! Where!" Quite

Chapter 3 Daily Verbal Communication

taken aback, nobody said anything for a moment until the most ingenious one among the visitors taking another look at the photo, said, "Oh, everywhere!"

Questions:

(1) What did the Chinese intend to mean by replying with "Where! Where!"?

(2) How did the Americans understand the reply?

(3) What would a Westerner say to respond to a similar compliment?

Ⅵ. **Activities**

1. Suppose you are preparing for post-graduation examination. A teacher of yours is introducing you to the Director of Admission. Initiate the conversation and ask for information about the requirements.

2. According to the Modesty Maxim proposed by Leech, people should minimize praise of self and maximize dispraise of self when addressing others. Chinese regard modesty as one of the most important virtues therefore there are great numbers of modest and honorific address forms in Chinese which are used widely by people. Please go to the library or surf the Internet to collect as much information as possible to fill in the table. Examples are given to you.

称呼对象	自称 谦称	他称 敬称	中性(平等关系)
自己/他人	余、吾、自、己、本人、鄙人、愚、	您、阁下	你、名字

3. Make a presentation on the differences of "gift-giving" and "gift accepting" between Western countries and China.

Ⅶ. **Video Watching**

《孙子从美国来》

Chapter 4 Verbal Communication

Among all factors of a language, it is the vocabulary that carries the most cultural information and reflects human life thoroughly. Seen from the perspective of social functions of a language, cultural distinction is the most prominent and widespread at lexical levels just like lots of culture-loaded words and proverbs existing in Chinese and English as well as different connotation of colors, numbers and animals between China and the Western countries. In addition, taboos, like some popular social phenomena, also convey different cultural information to all of us.

4.1 Culture-Loaded Words

4.1.1 Introduction

Culture-loaded words refer to the ones carrying some cultural connotation, which have a close connection with different cultures. Proverbs which have passed from generation to generation refer to some idioms, sayings or aphorism, having much to do with a national geographical environment, historical background, economic lives, customs, religious beliefs, psychological status and value systems. Fully understanding these culture-loaded words and proverbs, we can comprehend the target language very well. Otherwise, it will become a barrier for intercultural communication if we misunderstand those words.

It is commonly understood that culture-loaded words are culture-specific, that is, they depend very much upon a specific social or ecological setting, usually carrying more implication than non-culture-loaded words and belonging to a kind of associative reflection acquired and inherited by people of a group.

The communication between people from different cultures is a complicated process which usually involves their different life experiences. Although there is some universality existing in different cultures at present, differences are more extensive and influential in cross-cultural communication. And the striking differences between Chinese culture and Western culture result in the distinction of culture-loaded words. These cultural differences might be grouped as follows: (1) ecologically cultural differences; (2) socially cultural differences; (3) linguistically cultural differences; (4) materially cultural differences; (5) conceptually cultural differences. The five groups of differences may influence each other. Both the differences and the influences have been mirrored in the language. If a foreign language learner is not completely aware of the cultural difference, misreading the cultural information loaded in the words & expressions, errors will occur in the process of learning and communicating.

It is sometimes impossible or difficult to establish an exact equivalence of words between two languages. Thus the vocabulary vacancy appears, making our comprehension and translation rather difficult. For example, there is no corresponding term in English for Chinese term "风水". The reason is that in Chinese traditional culture, people will first survey the geographical features of a place before building a house or burying the dead so as to select an appropriate place to avoid the unluckiness and it is supposed that the location of a house or tomb has an influence on the fortune of a family. But in English-speaking countries, the dead is buried in the graveyard of the church without considering "风水"、Therefore, "风水" cannot find its counterpart in English. Similarly, there is no Chinese equivalent for cowboy or hippie—two well-known products of American society. The situation is similar to the words such as "京剧"、"武术"、"二胡"、"饺子" etc.

In addition, things or concepts are represented by one or perhaps two terms in one language, but by some more terms in the other language with finer distinctions existing. For example, the word "brother-in-law" is often used in our daily life, and it can be applied to someone's sister's husband, someone's husband's brother, and someone's husband's sisters' husband, which can be perceived to be different relatives in a similar way. And also the word "wife" has many translations in Chinese. Depending on the specific situation, it may be translated into "妻子"、"贱内"、"太太"、"夫人"、"老婆"、"爱人"、"爱妻"、"婆娘" and so on.

As well, terms with the same primary meaning may have secondary or additional meanings that differ remarkably from each other. Some color expressions are good examples to show it. We sometimes cannot directly translate some color words from one language to another without considering subtle changes in meaning. The English phrase "red-blooded" does not mean "红血的", rather, it is another way of saying that someone or his or her behavior is confident and strong. And the English phrase "red-eyed" just means someone has red eyes for lack of sleep. However, the Chinese equivalent "红眼" means at least two things: the literal meaning of red eyes, and the implied meaning that is similar to "green" in English, sharing the meaning of envy. There are some other examples such as "老黄牛"(a hard-working person) and "吃豆腐"(flirting with women).

4.1.2 Different Connotations of Colors, Numbers and Animals

As everybody knows, different cultures have different interpretation of colors, numbers and animals. Even when it comes to each of them, it will represent different meanings. As a result, it is necessary for us to learn about the distinction of them between different cultures.

1) Different Connotations of Colors

(1) Red

In Chinese, red usually has something to do with happiness, fortune, fervency, and auspiciousness, such as, 红喜字、红盖头、红地毯、红灯笼、红包、红利、满堂红。Also, red denotes the revolution such as 红旗、红领巾、红军、红色根据地.

In English red has something to do with blood or infelicity, implying bleeding, danger or violence. For example, red in tooth and claw (血淋淋), a red tag to the bull (令人生气的事情), be in the red (负债亏空), see red (大发脾气), red revenge (血腥复仇).

(2) Yellow

In Chinese, yellow has something to do with sovereign, harvest, and wealth. For example, 黄袍、黄榜、黄道吉日. Also it is related to something pornographic and scurrilous, such as 黄色电影、黄色小说、黄碟. In English, yellow just refers to a color existing in our life with the alerting function, such as, yellow card (黄牌)、yellow alarm (黄色警报)、yellow line (黄线)、yellow light (黄灯)、yellow page (黄页).

(3) Green

In Chinese, green is relevant to peace, safety, hope, environmental protection, such as 绿色食品(green food)、绿色产业 (green industry)、绿色能源(green power)、绿色产品(green products). Sometimes, it has something to do with the adultery between men and women, such as 绿帽子、绿头巾.

In English, green is the most popular color in the nature; also, it means immature, such as green tomatoes (不成熟的人). As well, green implies being jealous of somebody such as green with envy.

(4) White

In Chinese culture, white is an unlucky color, reflecting the Chinese preference or disgust in their material and spiritual world. In our daily life, white means being exhausted without blood or having no performance of life, symbolizing death or ill omen. During the revolutionary period, white was a symbol of being corrupt, reactionary, and backwardness. In addition it stands for failure, stupidity or having no profits. Finally, it has the meaning of being lack of knowledge or having no fame as well.

The symbolic significance of "white" in Western culture mainly focuses on its own color, such as the new snow, fresh milk and the color of lily. Westerners think white denotes grace and purity, so it is a popular color to most Westerners, signifying pureness and innocence. Also it is a symbol of integrity or honesty.

(5) Black

In Chinese culture, black has a strong sense of mystery as well as a solemn and serious tone. And its symbolic significance is more complex due to the influence of the Chinese traditional culture and Western culture. On one hand, it denotes faithfulness, bravery, uprightness and justice on the stage of the Chinese traditional opera; on the other hand, for most people they tend to have a feeling of being insidious, sinister and terrified naturally, thus black also represents evil, reactionary, crime or illegalness.

Black is the basic taboo color in Western culture with the meaning of rejection and obnoxiousness. It stands for death, ill omen, disaster, evil and crime, signifying shame and disgracefulness, frustration, anger and so on.

2) Different Connotations of Numbers

In China, three, six, eight and nine are usually regarded as the auspicious numbers, and these numbers or dates are usually used in our daily life. Also, nine is the largest one in the ten Arabic numbers with the partial tone for the Chinese character "久" meaning forever. Therefore, most emperors in China were fond of this number which could be reflected in the architecture of the Palace Museum. Also there are some other idioms related to nine in Chinese such as "九流"、"九泉"、"九族"、"九品"、"九连环"、"九牛二虎"、"九九重阳"、"九九艳阳天". As well, "three", "six", "eight" are also lucky numbers in Chinese culture. However, four and five have the partial tone with the Chinese characters "死" or "无". Therefore, these numbers are thought to be unlucky. In the West, thirteen is regarded as the unlucky number which is related to the story of the Jesus' death. If it is 13th on Friday, it is called the Black Friday, meaning the most unfortunate day.

3) Different Connotations of Animals

(1) Dragon

In Chinese culture, it is a totem with many royal associations, such as 龙床、龙袍、龙体、龙榻、龙心大喜、龙颜大怒. And all the Chinese people call themselves to be the offsprings of the dragon.

In Western culture, the dragon refers to a giant horrible animal like the lizard, meaning being terrible or disgusting. Therefore, in the West, to say a person is like a dragon usually implies that he is horrible, vicious and disgusting.

(2) Phoenix

In Chinese, it refers to an auspicious bird, implying that peace reigns in the whole world. Also it is the embodiment of the queen, such as 凤冠、凤辇. In English it means a kind of bird which has regenerated from the ashes after having been burnt to death. Therefore, phoenix means revival or regeneration in the Western country.

(3) Dogs

In the West, dogs are the faithful friends to the mankind and the lovable pets in the family. Therefore the idioms related to dogs usually have the positive meaning, such as "a lucky dog"（幸运儿）, "an old dog"（老手）, "Every dog has its day"（凡人皆有得意时）, "He works like a dog"（他工作很努力）, "Love me, love my dog"（爱屋及乌）. In China, dogs are insulting words, meaning being despicable and hateful, so the idioms related to dogs usually have negative meanings, such as 走狗、丧家犬、看门狗、狗急跳墙、狗仗人势、狼心狗肺、鸡鸣狗盗、蝇营狗苟.

(4) Owl

In China it has something to do with death, implying being unlucky; in the West, the owl relates to cleverness and wisdom. In the West, to say a person is like an owl suggests that he is as clever as an owl.

(5) Peacock

In China, it is an auspicious bird, so the peacock spreading its tail represents auspiciousness, prosperity and peace. However, in the West, the peacock usually stands for being pleased with oneself or showing off oneself. Therefore, to say a person is like a peacock suggests that he is as arrogant or self-conceited as a peacock.

(6) Bat

For the Chinese people, the bat is a symbol of being lucky, healthy and happy. Westerners don't love the bat, and they often associate it with a bad character. In their eyes bats can remind us of something ugly or something full of evil, sucking the blood of the animal. There are some idioms such as blind as a bat(有眼无珠), crazy like a bat(疯得像蝙蝠), have bats in the belfry(异想天开), be a bit batty(反常).

(7) Magpie

In China, the magpie is the symbol of auspiciousness and happiness. When it comes to magpie, people always think of the Double Seventh Day, which is associated with the love story of the Cowherd and the Weaver Girl. However, in the Western countries, the magpie is regarded as the symbol of being talkative. For example, "No wonder my phone bills are so high. When my daughter talks to her friends, she chatters like a magpie for hours. The girl is really a magpie."

4.2 Proverbs

Proverbs and idioms have inseparable connection with a national geographical environment, historical background, economic lives, customs, religious beliefs, psychological status and value system. Because of their close relationship with a particular language and culture, proverbs and idioms usually carry more implication than non-idiomatic expressions. If we want to understand their cultural connotation, we should take all the factors that affect their meanings into our consideration, so that we can fully understand proverbs themselves, especially the profound meaning they contain.

4.2.1 Proverbs Related to History

As we know, the social and historical development has had a huge impact on language. Taking English for an example, the evolvement of the proverbs can reflect the changes of the society and culture clearly. Therefore when we understand English proverbs, we need to consider their historical background and social development. Only through doing so, can we correctly understand the meaning of these proverbs. There are also long-standing cultural heritages in the Chinese history, which can be reflected in many proverbs such as "说曹操, 曹操到"(Speak of the devil, he appears)、"逼上梁山(be forced to do something desperately)"、"过五关,斩六将(experience many hardships)"、"新官上任三把火"(A new broom sweeps clean.).

With obvious national characteristics, these proverbs are closely related to Chinese history and culture. Some other examples are just like:

一箭双雕。Kill two birds with one stone.
欲速则不达。Haste makes waste.
勤能补拙。Works make the workman.
水滴石穿。Constant dropping wears the stone.
有其父必有其子。Like father, like son.
英雄所见略同。Great mind thinks alike.
留得青山在,不愁没柴烧。Where there is a life, there is a hope.
棒打出孝子,惯养忤逆儿。Spare the rod, spoil the child.

In 55 BC, the Roman commander Julius Caesar had conquered the British Isles, while the "Roman Conquest" began in 43 BC in the British history. From then on, the Romans occupied the Britain for 400 years. The influence of Roman culture on Britain has remained on the island since then; we can still find the trace of history in today's English proverbs. For instance,

(1) Rome was not built in a day.
罗马不是一天建成的。(喻指冰冻三尺,非一日之寒。)
(2) While Rome is burning.
大难临头依然寻欢作乐。(喻指对大事漠不关心。)
(3) All roads lead to Rome.
条条大路通罗马。(喻指殊途同归。)

These proverbs all show the assimilation of language and culture for a long time, reflecting such a fact that Roman Empire has brought great impact on the development of English.

4.2.2 Proverbs Related to Geography

The formation of proverbs is also closely related to people's geographical environment. The environment of local geography where people live and work has great influence on the formation of proverbs and proverbs in turn reflect the life and culture of people living in the special area. It's well known that Chinese culture is originated from the Yellow River, so there are many proverbs related to the Yellow River such as, "跳进黄河也洗不清"(It is difficult to make a convincing explanation no matter how a person tries to find an excuse.) and "不到黄河心不死,不撞南墙不回头"(Refuse to stop until all the hope is gone.).

Britain is an island nation, which is located on the British Islands between Western Europe and Atlantic Ocean, with the English Channel as well as the straits of Dover on the south and the North Sea on the east. Owing to the advanced oceanic transportation and fisheries, there are many proverbs about the voyages, fisheries, sea or water. For example,

Spend money like water. (挥金如土,而不是"挥金如水"。)

All is fish that comes to his net. (进到网里的都是鱼。)

The great fish eats up the small. (大鱼吃小鱼。)

He that would sail without danger must never come on the main sea. (谁在航行时不冒险,他就永远不要来到大海上了。)

Never offer to teach fish to swim. (不要教鱼儿游泳。这条谚语意为"不要在行家面前卖弄自己",相当于汉语谚语"不要班门弄斧"。)

People in the Great Britain live in a typical warm climate with temperate maritime, abundant rainfall, strong wind and fog. Then they have a proverb related to the particular weather, "It never rains but it pours". (不雨则已,一雨倾盆。)

4.2.3 Proverbs Related to Customs

Customs and habits reflect people's lives in a region. Proverbs not only reflect a nation's politics, economy, religion and literature, but also show its customs and habits. So there is a close connection between proverbs, customs and habits.

Every nation has its own favorite animals, so the favorite pets in different countries have distinctive characteristics. Generally speaking, "dogs" are derogatory words in the daily life of most Chinese people. For most Chinese people, dogs usually refer to dispicable persons or hateful things. But people living the Anglo-American countries are fond of dogs very much; they regard dogs as their reliable friends. As a result, in Anglo-American culture "dogs" often imply the positive meaning in most cases, and most proverbs about dogs don't have any derogatory sense except for the part affected by other cultures; instead there have been many proverbs with the commendatory sense about dogs.

Every dog has his own day.（每只狗都有它的好时光。）

The metaphor of this proverb is, "Everyone has a proud day".（人人都有得意时。）

Love me, love my dog.（喜欢我就要喜欢我的狗。）

It says, "Anyone who wants to keep the friendship with me needs to accept and stand all the things that belong to me, including my own hobbies and opinions." And it's similar to the Chinese proverb "爱屋及乌".

While in China, dogs tend to be regarded as annoying animals, which often stand for notorious men. So there are plenty of proverbs about "dogs" such as "狼心狗肺"（be as cruel as a wolf）, "狗咬吕洞宾,不识好人心"（Bite the hand that feeds them）and so on.

When it comes to cats, it's a different story. Chinese people are very fond of cats and they are usually regarded as the sweethearts by some people. However, in Western culture, a cat is often used to describe a spiteful woman such as "Cats hide their claws"（知人知面不知心。）.

4.2.4 Proverbs related to religion

Religious belief is not only a kind of ideology, but also a kind of culture. As a kind of spiritual custom, it is very complicated and related to human production, life, work and study. The Buddhism has been introduced to China for nearly two thousand years, and people believe that everything around the world can be dominated by the Buddha, so there are many proverbs containing "Buddha" and "Temple" in Chinese, such as "借花献佛（Offer a present to the guest with others' thing）"、"无事不登三宝殿（Never go to somebody's place except to ask for some help）", etc.

Christianity is one of the three major religions in the world. The new Christianity is viewed as Britain's national religion; although there are also many Catholic believers in Britain, the well-known Christian followers—Protestants account for the most proportion in Great Britain. Therefore, there are many English proverbs associated with Christian characteristics. For example:

If man proposes evil, God disposes of it.
上帝会阻止想要为恶的人。（喻指谋事在人,成事在天,或尽人事,顺天意。）
God helps those who help themselves.
上帝帮助那些帮助自己的人。（喻指自助者,天助之。）

Pay to Caesar what belongs to Caesar and God what belongs to God.
让上帝的归上帝,让恺撒的归恺撒。(喻指不在其位,不谋其政或做好自己的事。)

In Western countries, God is the creator of the world, so God in English takes high status in their daily life, which is proved in proverbs with high frequency.

In the right church, but in the wrong pew. 进对了教堂,但坐错了椅子。(喻义为"总的来说是对的,但细节上不对。")

The Bible is a great classical religious book, whose effect on the Western world is so enormous that no other works can compare with. Many legends in the Bible have exerted a great impact on Western culture. These legends in Bible have brought forth a large number of English proverbs, which have become an important part of the language and have been used widely.

The heart knows its own bitterness.
(一颗心知道它自己的痛苦,隐义为"切肤之痛"。)
Every man must carry his own cross.
(每个人必须背他自己的十字架,隐义为"自己的痛苦要靠自己来承受"。)

These proverbs come from the Bible, and the "cross" is the one to which Jesus was nailed when he was approaching to death with misery. So the word "cross" has the meaning of misery and these proverbs mean that "everyone must endure the sufferings in life and bear their own burdens".

"Forbidden fruit" is also a phrase from the Bible, and it is well-known to everyone. In the "Genesis", the apple that Adam had eaten in the Garden of Eden was called forbidden fruit. The implication in "Forbidden fruit" is that the forbidden thing one wants to get is always alluring.

Forbidden fruit is always sweet.
禁果是甜的。

4.2.5 Proverbs Related to Philosophy

Confucius, the founder of the Confucianism occupies an important position in the ideological field of China, and there are a large quantity of idioms or proverbs in the Confucianism works, such as "严于律己,宽以待人"(Be strict to oneself but more tolerant to others), "恭敬不如从命"(Obedience is better than politeness) and so on. Chinese proverbs also reflect some elements of Daoism like "福兮祸所伏,祸兮福所倚"(Misfortune may be a blessing in disguise) and so on. The Chinese traditional moral value emphasizes on "propriety, righteousness, benevolence, honesty", so there are some proverbs related to such moral qualities:

You can't have your cake and eat it too.
鱼与熊掌不可兼得。
It is a sin to steal a pin.
勿以恶小而为之,勿以善小而不为。
Many hands make light work.
众人拾柴火焰高。
Don't put off until tomorrow what you can do today.
今日事,今日毕。
Frank advice is like good herbal medicine, hard to take but ultimately beneficial.
良药苦口利于病,忠言逆耳利于行。
Look before your leap.
三思而后行。
When a person is in trouble, all the others around him come to help him.
一人有难大家帮,一家有事百家忙。
Helping each other enables the poor to become wealthy.
互帮互助,穷能变富。

The British have paid more attention to personal gains and losses. Such as:

He that has but only one eye must be afraid to lose it.
只有一只眼睛的人当然怕失去它,隐义为"不借钱给你,也是理所当然的"。
Lend your horse for a long journey; you may have him returned with his skin.
借马给人去远行,可能还你一张皮,隐义为"忘恩负义、恩将仇报"。
Lend your money, and lose your friend.
借出你的钱,失去你的朋友。

4.3　Taboos

Taboos are social cultural phenomena which refer to avoid doing something or talking about some topics in order not to make others feel embarrassed or offended. They are vehement (strong) prohibitions of some actions based on the belief those such behaviors are either too sacred or too accursed for ordinary individuals to undertake in fear of supernatural punishment. On a comparative basis, taboos, for example related to food items, seem to make no sense at all as to what may be declared unfit for one group by custom or religion may be perfectly acceptable to another. Generally speaking, taboos are usually used in the situations related to religion, sex, age, disease and death. As well, there are some taboos in the social communication and in some public situations such as the airport, the railway station, the library and so on. What's more, some taboos have something to do with numbers, colors, animals and plants in different cultures.

4.3.1　Religious Taboos

Different countries have different religious beliefs. Most Western people mainly believe in Christianity, including Catholicism and Eastern Orthodoxy, however, most Chinese are non-religious except that some believe in Buddhism and Daoism. People of Uyghur and Hui nationality are mostly Moslems.

Generally, Western Christians cannot worship the idol; also they cannot misuse the name of God; Indian Christians try to avoid holding wedding ceremony in the evening; Tonga's Christians tend not to leave home to work on Sunday. In some countries, people are overwhelmingly Roman Catholic and the influence of the Church is strong, with divorce and abortion still being strictly banned. In Lent they are not allowed to eat any animal meat except fish.

Chinese Buddhists are not allowed to drink alcohol, kill, and eat any meat. They can't marry and accept any property. The taboos for Daoist priests are similar to those for Buddhists. In Islam, all the Muslims are prohibited to eat pork and blood as well as drink wine. They are forbidden to give others gifts with animal logos. They tend to be stopped from entering the mosque in their shoes and touching food with the left hand.

4.3.2 Social Communicative Taboos

In the Western countries, it is necessary to make an appointment in advance for visiting someone, and people try to avoid a sudden visit because the sudden visit tends to disturb the host's schedule, which will cause lots of inconvenience. However, most Chinese used to pay no attention to making an appointment, which is viewed as lack of respect for each other in the business visit or the political visit. In our daily life, a sudden visit is not regarded as a serious infringement on the host's daily life; instead it is looked on as a pleasant surprise brought by a sudden visitor. In addition, the arrival time of an appointment is different between the Chinese and the Westerners. If the agreement is at 10 o'clock, for most Chinese, 10 o'clock is the ultimate deadline; the guests should arrive no later than ten o'clock, or they had better arrive a few minutes in advance, because the guests can't let the master wait for a long time; but for Westerners, it is better to postpone a few minutes later, because the host needs to get everything prepared.

In the conversation, Westerners refuse to involve personal privacy, such as age, income, marriage, love, property, degree of stoutness and so on. Personal privacy is placed at a higher position in Western culture, even the price of goods they have purchased is thought to be a privacy in the daily life. Through these we can see a cultural embodiment of the Western value—individualism and self-centeredness. In China, it is very normal to talk about income, age, marriage, stature and so on. In our daily life, we often confront such questions as "Where are you", "Where are you from" on the phone, even if we don't have a close relationship with the caller. In some rural areas, people tend to treat others as their friends and show their warmth and generosity without considering others' willing. In China, it is a taboo to talk about others' weaknesses in the conversation and it is impolite to point out others' faults or deficiency directly, instead it should be expressed tactfully if necessary.

In addition, when talking in public, Westerners are absolutely forbidden to speak loudly; they often make a quiet conversation in order not to affect other people. In China, it is common for people to speak loudly in public, and if they don't do so, they will not hear what others say. They have formed the habit of making a loud conversation, sometimes even in a quiet Western restaurant, they can't help talking and laughing loudly.

As well, Westerners tend to have a strict taboo about keeping a meter distance. In the crowded public places, people often observe such a rule strictly, keeping about one meter away from one another and avoiding participating in others' conversation. But In China, it is not necessary to think about such a taboo. When lining up, the distance between two persons is very short, even if they don't know each other at all.

4.3.3 Verbal Taboos

Verbal taboos refer to some words or expressions that are strongly prohibited in conversations. Just as violating cultural taboos can be quite offensive, so can verbal taboos.

English and Chinese have certain areas of agreement on taboo languages. Excreta and acts of human excretion (theses are euphemistic terms themselves) tend to be avoided in polite conversation. In English, if they must be mentioned, the terms should be expressed with the euphemistic ones. In Chinese, they are also taboos, but the Chinese attitude is less strict, and sometimes we hear people say "吃、喝、拉、撒、睡" in some serious public talks or conversations.

Talking about sexual intercourse and genital organs is also a taboo in both cultures. Since the "sexual revolution" of the 1960s in the U.S., the attitude toward sex in English-speaking countries has been freer and more open. Thus "to make love" or "to have sex with" are not uncommon in today's writing, some of which are slightly "dressed up" terms. What's more, the so-called "*four-letter words*" (e.g. fuck, tits, etc.) are still considered improper in most conversations, especially in some situations with females at present.

In many languages, swear words are taboos, which are generally true in both English and Chinese. In practice, some swear words seem to be more offensive than others, and using swear words in certain settings will be more unacceptable. In English, expressions like "Jesus Christ!", "Holy Mary!" and "Son of a bitch!" will be most unacceptable, whereas "Damn!", "Damn it!" and "Hell!" will be less so. Another usage will be the age, sex and occupation of the people involved. For instance, swearing a child will often bring a quick scold; swearing at a woman would be considered indecent; and swearing at a teacher would be regarded as highly improper behaviors. A third usage involves the setting or environment. The taboos are stricter in public speaking, in the classroom, or at the gatherings of people with certain social status.

As time goes by, people's reaction to swear words may undergo a certain change. Some swear words become rather common and gradually lose their original meanings; some are frequently heard in the young persons' conversation. For non-native speakers, though, it is better to be cautious when using profanities.

Exercises

I. **Questions for Discussion**

1. What is the definition of Culture-loaded words? Can you list some culture-loaded words both in Chinese culture and in Western culture? Please give some explanations respectively.

2. Do you know about some proverbs in our daily life or in the Western Culture? Please list as many as possible and give some necessary explanations.

3. Is it necessary or important for us to pay great attention to some taboos when we get along with our friends or family members? Why or why not? What about the foreigners? Can you give some explanations using one or two examples?

II. **Comprehension Check**

Decide whether the following statements are true (T) or false (F).

_____ 1. Culture-loaded words refer to the ones carrying some cultural meanings which have a close connection with different cultures.

_____ 2. In Chinese Culture, "墙头草" refers to the persons who have a strong will, never changing their minds easily.

_____ 3. In the Western culture, the green olive branch and the white pigeon are often regarded as the symbols of peace.

_____ 4. "A Juda's Kiss" tends to stand for happiness and fortune in most Western countries.

_____ 5. The English phrase "red-blooded" does not mean "红血的", rather, it is another way of saying that someone or his (her) behavior is confident and strong.

_____ 6. "Rome was not built in a day" means that we should start with the tiny thing if we want to achieve a great success in the future.

_____ 7. In the daily conversation, the Westerners are usually ready to answer some questions involving the personal privacy, such as age, income, marriage, love, property, degree of stoutness and so on.

_____ 8. White in the Western culture is similar to the color of the new snow, fresh milk and lily. Therefore it is a symbol of integrity, honesty, standing for purity and innocence as well.

_____ 9. Specifically speaking, Westerners will never mind eating the fat, the chicken or duck's skin, the animal's internal organs, the dog meat, the snake meat and so on.

_____ 10. On the first day of the first lunar month, it is a taboo for the Chinese to sweep trash, because they think it will take away the fortune from their houses.

Ⅲ. **Vocabulary**

Complete the following sentences with the words given below and each word can be used only once.

depend	offensive	prosperity	prominent	equivalence
represented	inseparable	reflect	appointment	unacceptable

1. Seen from the perspective of social functions of a language, cultural distinction is most _____ and widespread at lexical levels.
2. Because of the distinction between language and culture, it is sometimes impossible or difficult to establish exact _____ of words between two languages.
3. Things or concepts are _____ by one or perhaps two terms in one language, but by many more terms in the other language.
4. It is commonly understood that culture-loaded words are culture-specific, that is, they _____ very much upon a specific social or ecological setting.
5. Proverbs and idioms have _____ connection with a nation's geographical environment, historical background, economic lives, customs, religious beliefs, psychological status and value system.
6. Proverbs not only _____ a nation's politics, economy, religion, literature, but also show the nation's customs and habits.
7. In the Western countries, it is necessary to make an _____ in advance for visiting someone, and people try to avoid a sudden visit, because the sudden visit tends to disturb the host's working arrangement, which will cause lots of inconvenience.
8. In China, the peacock is an auspicious bird, so the peacock spreading its tail represents auspiciousness, _____ and peace.
9. The taboo is a special cultural phenomenon, which refers to a social custom to avoid doing that activity or talking about that subject, because people find them embarrassing or _____.

10. It is _____ for the British to send the white lily in the wedding ceremony because the white flowers always let people remember the hospital, the funeral and it is common to send the white flowers to the deceased person.

Ⅳ. Translation

Translate the following Chinese phrases into English and vice versa.

1. 吃豆腐
2. 铁公鸡
3. 爱屋及乌
4. 说曹操,曹操到。
5. 冰冻三尺,非一日之寒。
6. sit on the fence
7. an indifferent reception
8. Spend money like water.
9. Never offer to teach fish to swim.
10. Misfortune may be a blessing in disguise.

Ⅴ. Case Analysis

Case 1

One night a Chinese student majoring in English sat on the steps of the foreign students' residence and talked with two young male foreign students, one German and another American. They did not speak a word to her on their own initiative, but she asked many questions to get a conversation started. Every time they answered her with only one or two words. But she was determined to practice her English so she tried to keep the conversation going.

"How do you spend your weekend?" she asked.

The German boy answered immediately, "Fishing," and the two boys looked at each other meaningfully.

"Fishing?" She was really confused. "But where do you fish?" she asked.

"Fishing has two meanings. One is the literal meaning. The other is just sitting here or walking on the street and waiting for some girls to come up to us." Then they both burst out laughing.

She was annoyed. She sat there silently and then suddenly stood up and walked away without saying goodbye.

Questions:

What happened to the girl? Why did she leave without words suddenly?

Case 2

Sharing the Wealth

Anna Bilow had been working for a Chinese-owned and operated company in Nanjing for about six months. The division she was working in had a small collection of Chinese-English dictionaries, English language reference books, and some videos in English including a couple of training films and several feature films that Anna had brought at her new employer's request when she came from Europe. Anna knew that some of the other sections had similar collections. She had sometimes used her friendship with one of the women in another department, Gu Ming, to borrow English novels and reference books and in turn had let Gu Ming borrow books from her section's collection. On other occasions, she had seen friendly, noisy exchanges, where one of the other workers in her division had lent a book or video to a colleague from another section.

Anna thought it was a great idea when a memo was circulated saying that the company's leaders had decided to collect all the English language materials together into a single collection. The plan was to put them in a small room that was currently being used for storage so that all employees could have equal access to them. Now she would no longer have to go from department to department trying to find the materials she needed.

Anna was surprised to hear her co-workers complaining about the new policy. When the young man in charge came to the department to collect their English language materials, she was astounded to see them hiding most of the books and all but one of the videos in their desks. When she checked out the new so-called collection, she found that the few items were all outdated or somehow damaged. She also noticed that none of the materials she had borrowed from Gu Ming were in the collection. She asked her friend why the Chinese were unwilling to share their English language materials with all their co-workers, when they seemed to be willing to share them within their departments.

Questions:

What happened between Anna Bilow and Gu Ming? What made Anna feel confused in the above story?

Ⅵ. Activity

Surf the Internet and collect enough information, compare the social customs between China and the Western countries and make a presentation in front of class.

1. Differences in colors, numbers, plants and animals;
2. Culture-loaded words;
3. Proverbs;
4. Social communicative taboos;
5. Taboo languages.

Ⅶ. **Video Watching**

Princess《公主日记》

Chapter 5 Nonverbal Communication

5.1 Introduction

In the process of communication, language is not the only means by which people exchange information. Other ways also need to be involved in to help fully covey what we want to express. In conversation, for example, we express our ideas and feelings not only with words but also through voice tones, eye contact, postures, etc. Even clothing and hairstyle may send messages from one to another, although we might be unaware of it.

In the following scenario, Jim, Akira and Mitsuko interact. Akira and Mitsuko are exchange students from Japan who are spending a semester at an American college. Jim is an American student at the same college. Notice how each violates the others' expectations without realizing it. When reading the dialogue, keep in mind the different cultural orientations and the assumptions of nonverbal expectancy violations theory(违反预期理论).

Jim: (Nudges Akira and says loudly) This is a great party, eh?

Akira: (He is startled and tries to put some distance between himself and Jim.) Yes, thank you.

Jim: (Leaning forward toward Akira, with direct eye contact.) If you want to meet some girls, I could introduce you.

Akira: (Shocked by such an offer, he backs away.) But I don't know them. They might be upset.

Jim: Well, how else are you going to meet them?

Akira: (Uncomfortable) Maybe during a class or something.

Mitsuko, another Japanese exchange student, approaches Jim and Akira. She knows Akira, but not Jim.

Mitsuko: Hello, Akira. (Bows slightly and looks down.)

Akira: Ah, Mitsuko, this is my friend Jim.

Jim: Hi! (Forward leaning into her space.)

Mitsuko: Hi, Jim. (Bows slightly and does not make direct eye contact.)

Jim: Are you two friends? (Wondering why she won't look at him, thinks to himself, "Well, I'm not one of them, she probably thinks I'm ugly.")

Akira: Yes, we know each other.

A long pause ensues.

Jim: (Thinks to himself, "This is going nowhere—I've got to think of something to say." He speaks rather loudly.) Great party, hey guys?

Akira and Mitsuko both jump back.

Akira: (Thinks to himself "This guy is too weird.") Yeah, this is fun.

During this scenario, Jim violates Akira's kinesic, proxemics, paralinguistic, and haptic (触觉的) expectations. Notice in Lines 1 through 4 that Akira perceives that Jim is standing too close, talking too loudly, and thus backs away. From Akira's point of view, Jim violates his proxemics and paralinguistic expectations regarding haptics. From Jim's vantage point(优越地位), Akira violates his expectations as well, by not looking at him and not responding to his offer that he introduces him to women.

5.1.1 Definition of Nonverbal Communication

Language studies traditionally have emphasized verbal and written languages, but recently have begun to consider that communication involves both verbal and nonverbal behaviors. The study of nonverbal communication has only a relatively short history. There is no shortage of definition for nonverbal communication. Different scholars have made different efforts to define it. According to Judee K. (1996), the phrase "nonverbal communication" is "all those messages that people exchange beyond the words themselves". Some linguists also claim that nonverbal communication is communication without the use of words. Ruesch and Kees give a similar statement when saying that nonverbal communication indicates all communicative behaviors except oral speech. Other linguists take social conventions into account in defining nonverbal communication. Besides social conventions, many other factors are also important in helping convey nonverbal meanings such as the role of the environment, the message value of nonverbal stimuli and the communication setting, etc.

The definition of nonverbal communication differs from one expert to another. We propose that nonverbal communication involves all behaviors but words people use in when communicating with others.

Nonverbal communication expresses meaning or feeling without words. Universal emotions, such as joy, anger, and sadness, are expressed in a similar nonverbal way throughout the world while nonverbal differences across cultures may still be a source of confusion for foreigners. For example, feelings of friendship exist everywhere but their expression varies. In some countries, it may be acceptable for men to embrace each other and for women to hold hands while in other countries these displays of affection may be shocking.

What is acceptable in one culture may be completely unacceptable in another. Snapping fingers to call a waiter is appropriate in one culture but it may be rude in another. We are often not aware of how gestures, facial expressions, eye contact, and the use of space affect communication. In order to correctly interpret another culture's style of communication, great importance should be attached to nonverbal communicative competence in intercultural communication.

Researchers have shown that the words a person speaks may be far less important than the body language used when delivering verbal messages. Studies show that 55 percent of people's attitudes and feelings are communicated by the body, 38 percent by the voice and only 7 percent by spoken words. Apparently, we express ourselves more non-verbally than verbally.

5.1.2 Functions of Nonverbal Communication

Nonverbal communication has its own unique function in interpersonal communication. People cannot communicate fluently without nonverbal communication. We couldn't just miss them in regulating human interaction.

1) Repeating

Nonverbal messages are often used to repeat a point people are trying to make. We might hold up one hand waving a person goodbye while at the same time we actually use the word "Goodbye", or we might point in a certain direction after we have just said, "The new bookstore is just right to that building". The gestures and words have a similar meaning and reinforce one another.

2) Complementing

Nonverbal signals can modify or elaborate verbal messages. If you are telling a funny story, you may be smiling or laughing. When you tell someone that you are very pleased with his or her job, you can reinforce your satisfaction by patting the person on the shoulder at the same time, but this behavior is not allowed in some cultures.

3) Contradicting

Sometimes our nonverbal actions send signals opposite to the literal meanings contained in our verbal messages. You tell someone you still have some time, you can stay while you look at your watch frequently. On such occasions, we rely mostly on people's nonverbal messages to figure out what he or she really means.

4) Regulating

Nonverbal behavior is also used to regulate and manage verbal behavior. Direct eye contact and nodding are two typical nonverbal hints that mean "I want to talk" and "You can continue". Conversely, if we want to shut the channel up, we may decrease eye contact and perhaps keep silent. In short, our nonverbal behavior helps us control the situation.

5) Replacing

Nonverbal behavior can replace verbal messages. Gesture is a good way to do it. For instance, the classroom is quite noisy, you might place your finger to your lips instead of saying "Keep quiet". Nodding can also be interpreted as "I agree with you" or "Follow me" in most cultures. There's one thing that should be mentioned that nonverbal behavior can be interpreted differently in different cultures. Thus we should "do as the Romans do".

5.1.3 Classification of Nonverbal Communication

It is widely accepted in linguistic circle that nonverbal communication covers four areas: time language (temporal language or chronemics), space language (spatial language or proxemics), body language (body movement or kinesics), and paralanguage (voice modulation).

Each of these includes over twenty topics in a broad sense. The common topics most linguistic theorists address are as follows:

(1) time language: punctuality, promptness, time orientation, etc;
(2) space language: body distance and body touch;
(3) body language: posture, gesture, facial expression, eye behavior, etc;
(4) paralanguage: speed, volume, silence, pause, clothing, etc.

Having mentioned the nature of nonverbal communication, we can now turn to a brief examination of the cultural differences of nonverbal communication.

5.2 Time Language

Time is one thing people usually take it for granted. However, lack of awareness of the difference of time language will result in confusion and even frustration. People with a highly efficient living style could not bear the low pace of life in a country where time can be casually "wasted". Arriving two hours late for an appointment may be acceptable in one culture, whereas keeping someone waiting for fifteen minutes may be considered rude in another culture.

Because time is such a personal phenomenon, people perceive and treat it in a manner that characters. The way people treat time can also provide valuable cues to how members of that culture value and respond to time. This section will introduce some taxonomy(分类法) of time.

5.2.1 Time Orientation

Time is a fundamental basis on which all cultures rest and around which all activities revolve. Cultures vary due to different time orientations. Some ancient civilizations tend to look back because they have a long history to boast about, such as Greek, French, British and Japanese. They place much emphasis on tradition, since they have long histories that date back to thousands of years ago. They tend to use the past as a guide to make decisions and determine truth. Their time conception is past-oriented. Past-orientated cultures believe strongly in the significance of prior events. History, established religions, and tradition are extremely important to these cultures. Chinese culture is a past-oriented culture. This conception is well illustrated in some famous Chinese proverbs such as "Consider the past and you will know the present".

Present-oriented cultures like Filipinos and Latin Americans place emphasis on living for the moment. They tend to have a casual and relaxed lifestyle.

Future-oriented cultures encompass a preference for change. They have great faith in the better future. Americans basically belong to future-oriented culture. In the society, technological, social, and artistic trends change rapidly and affect people's lifestyles and their relationship. Independence and individualism are so much valued in America that they always drive them forward to build a brighter future.

5.2.2 Monochronic Time V.S. Polychronic Time

Each culture has its own attitude and practice relative to the use of time. According to Hall, "Time talks. It speaks more plainly than words." It's an important category of silent language. Cultures vary in the notion of time and the way to efficiently use it. Two of the most important time systems that relate to international business are Monochronic Time (M-Time) and Polychronic Time (P-Time).

As the word "monochronic" implies, this system views time as linear, segment and prompt. Generally, in monochronic culture people tend to do one thing at a time and may feel uncomfortable when an activity is interrupted. M-Time culture places great emphasis on schedules. Visitors who "drop by" without prior notice may interrupt the host's personal time and be considered impolite. Calling friends on the phone before visiting is an advocated social etiquette. People of M-Time culture think of time as something concrete and tangible. One can "gain time", "spend time", "waste time", "save time" or even "kill time". Northern American, Western and Northern European cultures are typical M-Time cultures.

M-Time culture highly values promptness. People are expected to keep appointments. Americans prepare carefully for business conferences, for personal interviews, for group meetings of all types. They assume this to be an elementary aspect of efficiency.

In contrast, P-Time culture emphasizes the completion of transactions and tends to be more human-centered rather than M-Time culture which rigidly adheres to the clock. P-Time is less rigid, less tangible and more flexible. People of this culture tend to do several things at the same time. A teacher may meet several students in the same room at the same time. A clerk may serve several customers at the same time. This may cause Westerners feel frustrated and sometimes they are even angry about it. Latin American, African, Arab and most Asian cultures are P-Time cultures. They emphasize people, human relationship and family more than schedules. They do not appreciate Western brevity so much. They would regard it as "coldness" and "haughtiness".

Offering and accepting invitations can also show the differences between two time systems. In America, an invitation for a dinner or a request for a date should be offered far in advance. This shows the honest desire of the host. If the invitations are some last minute decisions, they would be interpreted as insults. In some Arab and Asian worlds, however, the last minute invitations are acceptable and not to be considered as insults. The same is true in China. We Chinese seemingly prefer to go visiting directly at anytime we like without informing the hosts in advance. Only a few people make arrangements to make appointments before visiting. In answering an invitation, an American would let the host know whether he/she would accept it or not as soon as possible, thus the host could make preparation for it while people from P-time culture may just "forget" about the invitation. Accepting the invitation or not may depend on whether he/she is available that day.

Generally, M-Time is first of all characterized by cutting time into bits and scheduling one thing at a time. By contrast, P-Time culture schedules several things at a time so that the time allowed for each is quite flexible.

5.3 Spatial Language

Besides time, space is another way we use to convey messages. In daily life, people may use space to define interpersonal relationship. Consider the following expressions:

He is my bosom buddy.
Zhang Hong is a distant relative.
She kept him at arm's length during their first meeting.
The old man kept his distance from the visitor.
Nobody is nearer to his heart than his daughter.
He was once regarded as one of Li's closest friend.

Obviously, from the above expressions we find that body distance and body touch imply the distance of relationship. Close distance means intimate relationship while long distance implies the distant relationship.

5.3.1 Personal Space

Various cultures have their own body distance concept about comfortable zone in personal conversation. When two people are talking to each other, they tend to keep a specific distance apart. If someone pierces this boundary, the balance would be broken, and they will feel uncomfortable and try to move again to refind a comfortable distance.

Edward Hall classifies personal space into four categories: intimate zone, friend zone, social zone, and public zone (audience zone). The zone can vary according to personality and environmental factors, since an abnormal situation could bring people closer than they usually are. Each one demonstrates how space can communicate. Intimate zone is about 15 to 45 centimeters (6 to 18 inches). This is the most important zone of them all as it's only for a few selected people. The zone is reserved for lovers, children, as well as close family members, friends and pet animals. Anyone who is not meant to be in the intimate zone enters it will cause physiological changes (such as increased heart rate) in our body as we will feel threatened. Friend zone is about 45 centimeters to 1.2meters (18 to 46 inches). The distance is reserved for social gatherings such as parties, friendly interactions and so on. Social zone ranges from 1.2 meters to 3.6 meters (18 to 46 inches), reserving for strangers, newly formed groups, and new acquaintances. Public zone (audience zone) including anything over 3.6 meters (12 inches) is used for speeches, lectures, and theater. Public distance is essentially that range reserved for larger audiences.

In spatial language, Chinese and Arabic cultures have little regard for personal space. Chinese people do not care so much for their private space. When waiting in line to get the ticket or in front of a teller window, people tend to stand in close distance. They are so close that they can even smell the odor from each other or touch each other unintentionally. But they seem not to care. For native English speakers, personal space is important in their daily life in that they regard space as personal territory and how closely people position themselves in communication shows how intimate they are. That's why a Latin America feels an American cold while the latter feels the former is a kind of "pushy" when they talk with each other.

Space affects communication in many other ways. For instance, in the US, teachers prefer to arrange the desks to a circle for students to discuss, thus they can have the feeling of participation. While in China, teachers would rather students sit in rows to follow their orders.

5.3.2 Touching Behavior

Touch is a means of communicating through body contact. Used properly, it can enhance the feelings of warmth and trust in some cultures. Otherwise, it will cause annoyance and cultural conflict in other cultures. Anthropologists distinguish two broad categories of cultures according to touching behavior: touch culture and non-touch culture. Touch culture thrives on body touch. Non-touch culture is not rich in body touch. Axtell in *Gestures*(1998) classifies the following cultures as "touch" and "non touch":

Don't touch	Middle Ground	Touch
Japan the Untied States Canada Scandinavia Other Northern European countries	Australia Estonia France Ireland India Middle East countries China	Latin American countries Italy Greece Spain and Portugal Some Asian Countries Russia

Every culture defines its own touch customs. When Arabs talk, there is a lot of body touch, such as holding hands, patting, and hugging. In English-speaking countries, people try to avoid physical contact in conversation. If they touch others unintentionally, they would make an apology immediately such as "Sorry", "Oh, I'm sorry", or "Excuse me", because touching someone casually may cause unpleasant reactions.

In the West, hug is a sign of warmth and enthusiasm. It can happen between people of the same sex or opposite sex. It has no sexual connotation. While in China it has obvious sexual connotation, even lovers seldom hug in public. It is quite usual to see Chinese people of the same sex, especially females, walk hand in hand. While in America, friends of the same sex never keep such a close distance and such kind of behavior is considered homosexual there.

According to Axtell(1998), Chinese culture belongs to middle ground category. To adults, the closer their personal relationship is, more touch behaviours there would be. While Chinese attitude toward child is a different story. Many Chinese like to show their kindness or affection by fondling babies and young children: touching their faces, fondling their heads, even patting their buttocks. However, such behavior in Western culture would be considered rude, intrusive and offensive, and could arouse a strong dislike and even repugnance(厌恶). So the mothers of Wentern countries often stand by, watching in awkward silence, with mixed emotion, even when it is done by Chinese friends or acquaintances.

5.4　Body Language

The communicative function of the body means more than just hand or arm gestures. It refers to any little movement of any part of the body and also includes physical appearance. To better interpret body movements, we will categorize it into six important aspects: physical appearance, posture, gestures, facial expressions, eye contact and paralanguage.

5.4.1　Physical Appearance

Physical appearance is a universal thing. People from all over the world could not neglect it. There's a Chinese saying goes like "人靠衣装马靠鞍". In English a similar saying goes like "Fine feathers make fine birds". We all care much about the impression we leave on others, but what we focus on is different. In China, neat and clean dress is proper. There's no special rules for different occasions. BUT in Western countries, how to dress is an art.

One of my colleagues just comes back from her study as a visiting scholar in England. She shares her experiences:

I felt embarrassed that night. English staff there would like to give us visiting scholars a reception party. You know, it was a party. Since my major is English, I know something about their culture. I should have worn a dress there. I knew it. I should have, but I just neglected. You know, we Chinese seldom dress ourselves according to different occasions. I just wore my jeans there. And when I got there, I found I was the only lady who wore jeans rather than a dress. I felt so embarrassed that night.

In Western countries, people dress differently on different occasions. Generally, on a formal occasion, people need to dress formally such as suit, over-skirt, tie, etc. On an informal occasion, you can dress casual jeans or T-shirt. In some cultures, there are special requirements for women's appearance. In the Arab world, for instance, women should wear hijabs(面纱或头巾)which cover their faces.

Making-up is another thing women should pay attention to in intercultural communication. In China, women seldom use make-ups. But in Western countries, facial makeup is necessary for a lady. In Western culture, using makeups is considered a respect for others.

Generally, a neat look, a shaved face and a proper hairstyle are essential. They can leave someone with a positive impression. The physical appearance will play an important role in conveying messages about people's values, taste, status, age and occupation. A successful intercultural communicator must be the one who attaches great importance to his/her physical appearance.

5.4.2 Gesture

Gesture can be particularly troublesome, for a slight difference in making the gesture itself can mean something quite different from what is intended. One person's positive gesture may be another one's insult.

When an American makes the "V" gesture over his head, it means victory over some foe. This gesture is usually taken as a sign of victory after a boxer has defeated his opponent. However, this is a symbol of friendship in Russian culture. Thus, when Nikita Khrushchev, the leader of the USSR visited the USA in 1959, he raised his arms and made the "V" gesture above his head to show friendliness but it was misunderstood. Millions of Americans were irritated at what they interpreted to be an arrogant signal of confidence in eventual victory of communism over American capitalism.

1) Same Gesture Meaning Differently in Different Cultures

(1) "V" Gesture

Holding two fingers upright with palm and fingers faced outward.

In US, it is a signal for victory. In China, it means number two and victory as well. If used palm in, it has a crude connotation in England and South Africa.

(2) Thumb Up

In Britain or US, it means good, great or well-done and is also used asking for free ride. In German and Japan, it means Number one. In Persian culture it is highly offensive. In China it means great, good and you are wonderful.

(3) Thumb Down

In the U.S. and Canada, it shows disapproval. In Greece it is considered a rude sign.

(4) "OK" Sign

In most countries, it means "OK". In Japan and Korea, it signifies money. In France, it means zero. Among Arabs, accompanied by a baring of teeth, it means extreme hostility. In Latin American and Germany, it is considered obscene.

2) Different Gestures Referring to the Same Thing

(1) The Beckoning Sign

In the U. S, the gesture is shown as one palm up, fingers more or less together, and moving toward his or her body. In China, shaking the hand with the whole palm turned downward is the right way. In Philippines, it is a quick downward nod of the head. In German and much of Scandinavia, people will toss the head back. In most Arab countries, it is shown as holding the right hand out, palm upward, and opening and closing the hand.

(2) The Sign of "I'm very full"

In China, it is shown as one or both hands open, lightly patting one's own stomach. In America, it is shown as raising one hand to throat with extending fingers and palm down (often with the remark "I'm full up to here").

Head movements also differ culturally. In India and Bulgaria, for example, to signify no, people may nod their heads and shake their heads to say yes, which is much different from that in Chinese culture and most other cultures all over the world. So gestures can be very confusing inter-culturally. But some gestures have the universal meaning such as, a kiss means love, a smile means friendship, and a clenched fist typically indicates hostility or aggression.

Not all gestures can find equivalents in another culture. For example, when expressing the idea of warning not to do something, or indicating that what the other person doing is wrong, an American raises and wags his or her forefinger with one hand, with other fingers clasped. The raised forefinger is wagged from side to side. This gesture does not exist in Chinese culture though some Chinese understand the meaning of it. In China, if we want to show our thanks, we can salute with the hands folded. This gesture could not be found in other cultures.

5.4.3 Posture

Posture can send positive or negative messages in communication. It refers to the general way people sit, stand, walk or lie. Each culture has its own distinctive nonverbal cues despite of universal ones. It's true that posture offers insight into a culture's deep structure, which may cause confuse in intercultural communication.

In Western countries, in conversation, the people who stand usually means he is in the position of a higher social status, a higher position in the company or elder than his interlocutor. In their interaction, he plays the leading role. Thus, he may stand or walk up and down to decide the process of conversation. While in China, people do differently. In China, people stand up to show respect when they are introduced to others, whereas in certain Polynesian cultures, people sit down. In America, when answering the teachers' questions, the students can just remain sitting. He/She is not obliged to stand up. But in China, to show the respect for teachers, students usually stand up to answer teachers' questions. Standing with arms akimbo is common in America with neutral meaning. Such a posture may be adopted both by men and women. Women adopt this posture to show their impatience. However, such a posture in China is a signal to protect oneself from being approached.

Sitting posture is a constant source of cultural misunderstanding. In China, there's a saying goes that "站如松,坐如钟"(Stand as straight as a pine and sit as upright as a bell.). Chinese value proper stance and sitting position, and the old-fashioned wooden armchair is to meet such a culture requirement, while English people and Americans are not used to the sitting position. In America, consciously or unconsciously people often slouch when they stand or fall into chairs putting their feet on their desks or sit cross-legged. In doing so, they believe they are in a more friendly atmosphere. Whereas, in the eyes of Chinese, it's kind of domineering(盛气凌人) posture. Thai and Arabs take it as an insult. In their cultures, the sole is the lowest part of the body, and should never be exposed in front of others. In Germany and Sweden slouching is considered a sign of rudeness and poor manners.

Western culture emphasizes "ladies first". So gentlemen would like to wait until ladies sit down. And before that, a gentleman would help pull the chair for the lady first. But in Chinese culture, we respect for seniority. Most of the time, people will wait until the elders be seated.

The case in classroom also differs in the two cultures. In an American classroom, we may see a teacher sitting on the desk, putting his/her feet on chairs. In doing so, they just mean to create a relaxed atmosphere for the students to take part in classroom activities. However, this could never happen in a Chinese classroom. If doing so, the teacher would be considered as halfhearted, casual and in-disciplined. And such behavior would be considered harmful to the teacher's image. His/her qualification as a teacher would be doubted.

From the above differences, people may note the values, norms, and beliefs or subjective culture of a particular group reflected in the nonverbal codes. In the United States, the emphasis is upon comfort and people seem to have a loose and easy stance, but Chinese culture values a rigid, erect and quiet stance.

5.4.4 Facial Expression

Facial expression conveys people's emotions. Universal emotions, such as happiness, fear, and sadness, are expressed in a similar nonverbal way throughout the world. However, the use of facial expression is different culturally, and it may cause a lot of confusion for many foreigners. For example, Latin and Arab cultures use more intense facial expressions. It is common to see men crying in public in many Mediterranean countries. Americans usually suppress their sadness. Whereas East Asian cultures use more subdued facial expressions. Japanese tend to hide their expressions of anger, sorrow or disappointment with laughing or smiling. Chinese people often control their emotions, too.

However, a facial expression may convey more than one message. For example, smile in China has many meanings: both positive and negative meanings. Westerners often complain that Chinese people smile at them in an improper situation. An American colleague tells me that in her class, when students are asked to answer questions, they sometimes make no response, just stand there and smile. She feels so confused and frustrated. When I explain to her that the students just use smile to conceal their embarrassment for not being able to answer her questions, she's relieved. Chinese people are so kindhearted and caring that sometimes they want to use smile to help people out of the awkward situation. But it is often taken wrong by Westerners. Another story is that an American was parking his bicycle and the bicycle accidentally fell over. He felt embarrassed. At that time, he found a Chinese passerby looking at him with smile, he felt quite angry and humiliated. He just couldn't understand why the Chinese laughed at him. In fact, the Chinese passerby just smiled to tell him not to take it serious but laugh it off or it's nothing serious, etc.

Smile is a universal facial expression, but why we smile, to whom we smile, and when we smile often differ from culture to culture. In Japanese culture, smile is used to mask emotion or avoid answering a question. Too much smile is perceived as the sign of a shallow person in Korean culture. The French smile for an explicit reason. In Germany, smile is reserved for friends. Thais smile much of the time, and Thailand is called "the Land of smile".

Facial expression is the major means to show one's emotion, to demonstrate interpersonal attitude and to provide nonverbal feedback on the comments of others. To avoid serious misunderstanding, people who engage in intercultural communication should learn to interpret facial expressions appropriately.

5.4.5 Eye Contact

"The eyes are the window to the soul.", "Eyes speak.", these sayings indicate that from people's eyes we can see a lot. A person's eyes reveal how people feel, or what they think, whether they are interested in something or not, etc. Nevertheless, different cultures have different eye contact "rules": to look or not to look; when to look and how long to look, who to look at, etc. Only when we know the unique social rules can we make the intercultural communication a perfect one.

There is a popular motto "Never trust a person who can't look at you in eyes". In British, North American and Northern European cultures, eye contact is the sign of openness, trustworthiness and integrity. Constant eye contact ensures that the conversation partner is interested in the topic. The lack of eye contact means rudeness, impoliteness, contempt, and bad manners for native English speakers. However, staring at someone is not polite.

A foreign colleague once complained to me: "Chen, I don't know what to do. In my class, when I give lectures to my students, they seldom look at me. They usually look at the screen or just look at the platform. They seldom have direct eye contact with me. Once I look in the eyes of them, they just move away their eyesight. Are they dissatisfied with my lecture? Or are they simply not interested in my topic?"

I told her there was nothing wrong with both of them. They have just both neglected the cultural differences between the two countries. When communicating with others, Chinese speakers avoid prolonged eye contact and use less eye contact than Americans do, to show respect, politeness, and compliance, especially in conversation with people of higher social status. However, in the process of conversation, the short time of eye contact makes native English speakers often think that Chinese people are not interested in what they say. They may think Chinese people are insincere and dishonest. On the other hand, Chinese people feel that native English speakers always stare at them, which make them feel uncomfortable and annoyed.

To look at someone in the eyes in Japan is rude, because they believe the behavior is an invasion of others' space, cause they are taught to look at the neck. While for Arabs, frequent eye contact is necessary in conversation. Even when two persons are walking while chatting, they would stop to face the partner and speak. In order to see the eyes of speakers more clearly, Arabs will move closer, which would make non-Arabs feel uncomfortable. In Muslim countries, women and men are not supposed to have eye contact.

In short, rules governing eye contact are different from culture to culture. Very direct eye contact can be misinterpreted as hostility, aggressiveness, or intrusiveness while the intended meaning is a signal of interest. Minimal eye contact may be misunderstood as lack of interest or dishonesty, fear, or shyness while in fact, it is a sign of respect or obedience.

5.5 Paralanguage

Paralanguage is a component of meta-communication that may modify nuance meaning, or convey emotion. According to the *American Heritage Dictionary of the English Language* (2003), paralanguage means "speaking tempo, vocal pitch and intonational contours(语调升降)". When people talk, they do not use the same monotonous tone, volume, or speed. There are individual and ethnic differences. When the doctor tells a patient that he will be OK with certain treat in a firm tone, the patient will utter a sign of relief. If you ask an obviously depressed person "What's wrong", and he answers, "Nothing, I'm fine", you probably won't believe him. When an angry person says "Let's forget this subject, I don't want to talk about it any more!", you know that he hasn't stopped communicating. His silence and withdrawal continue to convey emotional meaning. So, paralanguage includes such nonverbal voice quality as tone, tempo, pitch, volume and silence. Paralanguage may be expressed consciously or unconsciously.

Vocal Pitch measures whether a voice is low or high. People may voice from a whisper in intimate talk to a high pitch in screaming. Compared with women's pitch of 220HZ, men speak in a higher pitch about 120HZ. Studies show that low-pitch speaking voice, both for men and women, is preferred by the listeners. Whether deserved or not, low-pitch talkers are associated with authority, credibility, strength and self-confidence. High-pitched voice, on the other hand, is less pleasant to the ears of the listeners. It gives the illusion of a lack of confidence and makes the person sound insecure, weak, nervous and less truthful.

Tempo in speech also illustrates cultural variation. According to British phonetician Daniel Jones, there is a striking difference between British and American English in speech tempo. He finds that the British speak a hundred syllables more than Americans per minute. The underlying cause may be that British people use a lot more reduced syllables than Americans. The Voice of American and the British Broadcasting Corporation programs may well prove the difference.

Difference in tempo also exists between American speech and Chinese speech. Chinese TV and radio speakers are far slower than their American counterparts. The underlying causes of this marked difference may be explained in two ways. One is that speech tempo tends to increase with the development of industry. Industrialized countries have a faster speech tempo than non-industrialized countries. The other is that the English language has much more polysyllabic words and carries less information per syllable than the Chinese language does. That is to say, the same amount of information can be contained in fewer Chinese syllables. Therefore, Chinese speech can afford to be slower than American speech.

Volume refers to the power of loudness of your voice. Generally speaking, a loud voice is used in shouts and quarrels to express anger. It is often perceived as aggressive or overbearing. Soft-spoken voice is often regarded as timid or polite. Volume differs in different situations. A soft voice is used in persuasion, consolation, telephone conversation and job interview. In interpersonal communication, the loud volume of an excited person is often interpreted as connoting aggressiveness, loss of self-control, or even anger.

Volume differences are culture specific and gender specific. Americans are skilled in regulating their voice volume and employ different volumes depending on the size of the audience and the physical environment, while people in Asian countries lack comparable skills. To show strength and sincerity, Arabs prefer very loud voice. Germans conduct their business with a commanding tone that shows authority and self-confidence. In Japan, raising one's voice often implies a lack of self-control.

All in all, paralanguage, with the elements of tone, tempo, pitch and volume, should never be underestimated. A good knowledge of paralanguage will help you to correctly interpret another culture's style of communication.

Exercises

I. Questions for Discussion

1. What are the major differences between Chinese and American nonverbal communication?
2. What are the contents of chronemics, proxemics, kinesics, and paralanguage?
3. What is paralanguage? Is it important for intercultural communication?
4. Since volume can send messages, what messages can volume convey?
5. What are the major differences between verbal and nonverbal communication?

II. Comprehension Check

Decide whether the following statements are true (T) or false (F).

_____ 1. Americans and Chinese have very different ways in manipulating volume of speech.

_____ 2. People have a full understanding of the importance of paralanguage in communication.

_____ 3. Gestures can be particularly troublesome. A positive gesture in one culture may be an insult in another culture.

_____ 4. Speaking is just one mode of communication. There are many others.

_____ 5. People in all cultures use nonverbal gestures to communicate consciously.

_____ 6. Latin American, African, Arab and most Asian cultures are M-time cultures.

_____ 7. Arabs belong to touch culture.

_____ 8. In some cultures, eye contact should be avoided in order to show respect or obedience.

_____ 9. Nonverbal communication is used only as a means of substituting for verbal communication that cannot adequately convey an intended message.

_____ 10. Nonverbal communication is the process of communication through body language.

III. Vocabulary

Complete the following sentences with the words given below and each word can be used only once.

fondle	slouch	paralanguage	posture	gesture
obedient	volume	genuine	hospitable	bewilder

1. The beautiful thing in the world often makes one _____ admiringly.

2. This button is for adjusting the _____.

3. _____ is the use of manner of speaking to communicate particular meanings.

4. The artist asked his model to take a reclining _____.

5. Don't _____! Stand up straight!

6. She _____ her disappointment by laying her hand on her forehead.

7. One of my colleagues explained to her that China is a _____ nation.

8. She was totally _____ by his sudden change of mood.

9. I was no longer a sweet _____ little boy.

10. If this offer is _____, I will gladly accept it.

Ⅳ. Translation

Translate the Chinese phrases into English and vice versa.

1. 眼睛是心灵的窗户

2. 沉默是金,雄辩是银。

3. 人靠衣装,马靠鞍

4. 站如松,坐如钟

5. 与时俱进

6. Silence means more than words at this very moment.

7. First come, first served.

8. If you drink with a bosom friend, a thousand cups are not enough; if you argue with someone, half a sentence is enough.

9. Time is money.

10. A real man never goes back on his words.

Ⅴ. Activities

1. Suppose you are an exchange student in America. One of your American friends invites you to his/her house for his/her birthday party. Try to use some specific examples to show different ways of nonverbal communication in such an intercultural situation. Role-play with your partner.

2. Suppose you are going to invite your American friends out to dinner, what is the proper way to book a table and send your invitation to your American friends?

Ⅵ. Case Analysis

Case 1

Situation 1

In a Chinese classroom a girl was asked to answer a question. She stood up and smiled, without making any sound.

Situation 2

When an American was parking his bike and the bike accidentally fell over, he felt embarrassed. While those Chinese people around just looked at him and laughed.

Situation 3

In the dining room, when an American dropped a plate quite by accident and felt bad, and Chinese onlookers laughed, compounding his discomfort and causing his anger and ill feeling.

Question for discussion:

Could you explain the meaning of smile or laugh in each case?

Case 2

Li Lan had an American friend Susan. They usually had lunch together and Li Lan often asked Susan for advice on problems she faced adjusting to American society. Susan gave Li Lan a lot of advice and helped her to improve her English. Once Li Lan needed urgently a big sum of money to pay her tuition fee. Since she has no other friends in the States, she turned to Susan for help and promised that she would return the money soon. To Li Lan's great disappointment, this time Susan didn't seem happy to lend the money to her. Though Li Lan returned the money as she promised, they didn't get along well from then on.

Question for discussion:

How would you explain Susan's behavior toward Li Lan?

VII. Video Watching

Lie to me《别对我说谎》

Chapter 6 Social Customs and Etiquette

6.1 Introduction

Collins Online Dictionary defines custom as an activity, a way of behaving, or an event which is usual or traditional in a particular society or in particular circumstances. It is a long-established practice, which is considered to be unwritten law, resting for authority on long consent. Social customs are the social infrastructures for human actions and interactions by which we live our lives and decide what is important in our lives. They are closely related to cultures, composing various traditions and social norms which are passed from generation to generation. Customs are not static. They will evolve and change, then bring about the social progress, and reshape themselves over time.

Etiquette refers to the customs or rules governing behaviour regarded as correct or acceptable in social or official life. They are the forms, manners, and ceremonies established by convention in social relations, in a profession, or in the official life. According to *Wikipedia*, etiquette is defined as a code of behavior that delineates(描绘) expectations for social behavior according to contemporary conventional norms within a society, social class, or group. Generally speaking, etiquette codes prescribe and restrict the ways in which people interact with each other, based on the respect for other people and the accepted customs of a society.

Social customs and etiquette are important parts of all cultures. They reflect different life styles, social values and spiritual pursuits in a certain culture. Most of Chinese traditional social customs and etiquette are originated from Confucianism, Daoism, and Buddhism, whereas the western social customs are mostly related to religions. Getting to know the social customs will lead you to gain insights into different cultures.

In this chapter, we will introduce the different social customs in China and the western countries from the following two aspects. Firstly, we will talk about different festivals between China and some western countries, including their origin, their evolving process and their festival customs and so on. Then we will give an elaborate explanation on the distinction of some customs relevant to the life growth in China and the western countries, for example the baby's birth, the birthday celebration, the grown-up ceremony and the marriage.

6.2 Traditional Chinese and Western Festivals

Traditional festival is a very important part of culture. It is not only a way of showing people's social life, but about how to pass on the culture from one generation to another. With the development of culture interaction, we know lots of western festivals, and we even celebrate some of them. When celebrating these festivals, we can find out some differences between them.

6.2.1 Spring Festival VS Christmas

1) Spring Festival

Chinese Spring Festival, or Lunar New Year, is said to be existed for more than 4,000 years. It is the greatest festival for the Chinese families to get reunion. According to the folk, this traditional holiday actually lasts from the twenty-third day of the twelfth month to the fifteenth day of the first month (Lantern Festival) in the lunar calendar, which can be roughly divided into three periods: the days before the festival, the festival celebrations and the days after the festival, with various rituals conducted in each phase.

2) Preliminary Eve

The twenty-third day of the twelfth lunar month is regarded as Preliminary Eve, or *Xiaonian* Festival, when people used to offer sacrifice to the Kitchen God (The people in southern China celebrate it on the twenty-fourth). The Kitchen God is one of Chinese domestic Gods who protect people's health and their family. It is believed that on that day, just before Chinese New Year, the Kitchen God returns to Heaven to report the activities of every household over the past year to *Yu Huang*, the emperor of the heaven, who either rewards or punishes a family based on this report. *Xiaonian* Festival marks the start of the countdown as the festivities begin to gear up for Spring Festival. There are some very old customs to celebrate the day, like pasting couplets on either side of doors, worshiping the "Kitchen God", and sweeping houses.

(1) Cleaning and Purchasing

Before the Lunar New Year's Day, Chinese families will do the thorough spring-cleaning, They will sweep up the grounds, the walls, and every corner of the house thoroughly. The origin of this ritual is that in Chinese, the pronunciation of "dust" resembles that of the word "old" (Chen). Therefore, cleaning means a farewell to the bad luck or the old stuff to usher a new start.

Meanwhile, people tend to buy new items, especially new clothes for the coming festival, which is a symbol to welcome new things and get ready for the new year.

(2) Couplets

Chinese couplets, also called *Dui Lian*, are usually pasted on the front door as a symbol to celebrate the New Year. The history of couplets can be traced back to the ancient *Taofu*, which is a piece of peach wood used to protect against evil spirits in ancient time. Then, in Song Dynasty, people began to write some antithetical couplets on the wood to express good wishes. Gradually, the peach wood was replaced by the red paper with two lines of hand written poetry in matching metrical form. And a pair of complete couplets include the antithetical on both the right and left side of the door and a horizontal scroll hanging on the lintel(楣,过梁) of the door.

(3) Upside down "Fu" and Paper-Cutting

The character *Fu* means good fortune in Chinese, symbolizing people's good wishes for the future. Therefore, most Chinese people tend to paste it on the gates or on the walls during the Spring Festival. The character *Fu* is usually pasted upside down, pronouncing the same as fortune (福到) in Chinese. This convention is widely accepted among Chinese. In addition, paper-cutting is an art form that involves cutting (usually red) paper. The most popular subjects are animals, humans, flowers, or the character of *Xi* or *Fu*, which means happiness. During Chinese New Year, most paper-cutting pieces are pasted on windows, but some are pasted on the walls or the front doors.

(4) New Year's Eve & New Year's Day

The two occasions are regarded as the peak of the whole Spring Festival which has been embodied by some typical activities such as the family reunion dinner, staying up all night, setting off firecrackers and so on. Besides, visiting relatives is indispensable during the first day of the New Year.

(5) Family Reunion Dinner

The family reunion dinner is the most important feast for Chinese families, and especially for those who are far away from their home. With all the family members sitting around the table and toasting best wishes to each other, the whole family is surrounded by the warm festive atmosphere. During the dinner, normally some dishes such as fish, tofu, meatball will be served to signify prosperity and reunion.

(6) Staying Up

The custom of staying up all night can be traced to the Northern and Southern Dynasties. It was said that there was a frightening demon called "Nian". On every New Year's Eve, the demon would come out to eat people, animals, and did great damages to properties. Therefore, on the New Year's Eve, people would have the lights on and stay up for the entire New Year's Eve to keep the demon away.

(7) Lucky Money

Lucky money is the money that is traditionally given in red packages to young people. Chinese people consider red as the color of luck and happiness, so they usually use red envelopes decorated with symbols of wealth and luck to express their best wishes for the young. The money inside may be given in the from of coins or bills. Children may use theirs to buy small toys and candies, while elder children may use it for school supplies or even save some for tuition.

(8) Firecrackers and Fireworks

On the New Year's Eve, most Chinese tend to set off the firecrackers at 12 o'clock at the midnight to welcome the arrival of the new lunar year. The custom is said to be associated with a fierce monster *Nian*(year), which was believed to eat the human beings. At the beginning, people were scared of it, so they hid themselves on the evening when the creature came out. Later on, it turned out that "Nian" was afraid of the red color, the fire and the loud sound. Accordingly, people threw bamboo into the fire to drive the monster away. After the invention of gunpowder, bamboo was replaced by firecrackers nearly 2,000 years ago. In the traditional culture, celebrating the Spring Festival is also named *Guonian* (meaning "celebrating the year") and the customs such as pasting the red couplets and setting off fireworks have lasted till today.

(9) Eating Jiaozi

Jiaozi is the typical food during the Spring Festival especially in the northern China. Made of flour and stuffed with different kinds of meat or vegetables, *Jiaozi* are usually shared by the family members on the Spring Festival Eve. Resembling *Yuanbao*, the money used in Ancient China, *Jiaozi* are considered to bring people a good fortune in the coming year. Sometimes, people tend to put coins, candies, peanuts, or chestnuts randomly in some dumplings, and the people who accidentally eat them are believed to be the luckiest one that will be blessed in the new year. In addition to the New Year's Eve, it is also a convention in many regions of China for people to eat dumplings on January 1st and 15th of the lunar calendar.

3) Christmas Day

Christmas, the day to honor the divinity of Jesus, is the most important festival in most western countries. For modern Christians, it just originates from the birth of Jesus Christ, as written in the Bible. Christmas is also a good time for families to get together in that it is very similar to Chinese Spring Festival reunion.

(1) Santa Claus

The prototype of Santa Claus is believed to be Saint Nicholas, Bishop of Myra—a place in Turkey, who was generous and particularly benign to children. Throughout Europe, he served as the patron of various kinds of people. For instance, in Greece, he was the patron of sailors; in France, he became the patron of lawyers; and in Belgium, he was regarded as the patron of children and travelers. In addition, numerous European churches were dedicated to him, the Feast of St. Nicholas, was invented in his honor some time around the 12th century, which was celebrated on December 6 featuring gift-giving and charity.

(2) Christmas Trees

In the 16th century, it became a custom to decorate fir trees both indoors and outdoors, with apples, roses, gilded candies, and colored lights in Germany. A fir tree hung with apples was viewed as the Paradise Tree, representing the Garden of Eden. In addition, Protestant reformer Martin Luther was said to be the first person to adorn trees with light.

It was Queen Victoria's husband, Prince Albert, who brought the notion of Christmas tree to England in 1848. The well-known picture of the Royal Family of Victoria in which Albert and their children gathered around a Christmas tree in Windsor Castle, contributed to the popularization of the tree throughout Victorian England. Brought to America by the Germans in Pennsylvania, the Christmas tree eventually got popular with Americans in the late 19th century.

(3) Christmas Stockings

In the western countries, it is said that St. Nicholas is a generous and warm-hearted old person who is ready to lend a warm hand to the persons in need. When Christmas Day comes, he is said to ride his white horse to arrive at the nobleman's house, throwing small bags of gold coins contained by the stockings down the chimney, which are hung by the fireplace to dry.

6.2.2 Double Seventh Day VS Valentine's Day

1) Double Seventh Day

Chinese Double Seventh Day, the seventh day of the seventh lunar month, also known as Qixi Festival, is what Valentine's Day means to the Westerners. It has much to do with a popular folk love story—the Cowherd and the Girl Weaver, endowing the festival with some romantic elements.

It is said that the Cowherd, Niu Lang, is a kind-hearted boy who accidentally takes good care of a sick cattle from the heaven. To express his gratitude to the Cowherd, the cow helps him married a fairy, Girl Weaver(Zhi Nü) and live a happy life. However, the king of the heaven disapproves of their marriage, sending the Empress of Heaven to take the Girl Weaver back. With the help of the cow, the Cowherd flows to the heaven together with his two children, trying to catch up with his wife. Unfortunately, when the Cowherd and his children are about to reach the Girl Weaver, the Empress takes off the gold hairpin from her head, drawing a line in the sky. Immediately, an immense celestial(天空的) river appears between the Cowherd and the Girl Weaver, separating them from each other forever. In face of such a huge river, the couple can do nothing but sheds their tears unceasingly, which wins sympathy from the queen in the end. Eventually, she permits them to meet only on the seventh day of the seventh lunar month every year. Tens of thousands of magpies are moved by their love story, coming to build a bridge for them to meet each other. Gradually, the day that the Cowherd and the Girl Weaver meet every year has become the Double Seventh Festival.

On the night of Double Seventh Day, girls will sew some articles to compete with each other in rural regions. In addition, they prepare some sacrifices to worship the Girl Weaver in the hope of being endowed with the masterly sewing skill and meeting their future sweethearts as well. Although some conventional customs have changed a lot or even disappeared, the legend of the Cowherd and the Girl Weaver has been passed down from generation to generation.

2) Valentine's Day

In some western countries, Valentine's Day falls on February 14th and it is a festival for people to convey their love with greetings and gifts. It is said to be associated with a priest named St. Valentine who was martyred about 270 A. D. by the emperor Claudius II Gothicus. According to the story, the priest signed a letter to his jailer's daughter whom he had fallen in love with "from your Valentine". Another version is that the holiday is associated with Lupercalia, a Roman festival held in mid-February. The festival was primarily to celebrate the arrival of the spring, including fertility rites and the pairing game between women and men by the means of lottery. At the end of the fifth century, Pope Gelasius I replaced Lupercalia with St. Valentine's Day, the festival then evolved into the one related with romance almost ten centuries later.

When Valentine's Day comes, it is common for the young to send some gifts such as valentine cards, chocolates and red roses to their sweethearts, symbolizing beauty and love. Such a festival is very popular in the western countries such as United States, Britain, Canada, and Australia; and it is also celebrated in other countries, including France and Mexico. In recent years the holiday has also become prevalent in some Asian countries like China and Japan.

6.2.3 Qingming Festival VS Halloween

1) Qingming Festival

Qingming Festival, also known as Pure Brightness Festival or Tomb-sweeping Day, is one of the traditional Twenty-four Solar Terms in China, falling on either April 4th or 5th of the solar calendar. It is typically a turning point that the temperature begins to go up, and the rainfall starts to increase gradually. Also it is an indication for the spring plowing and sowing. Besides being a seasonal symbol, it is an important moment to pay respect to the dead. And in the modern times, also it is an appropriate time for a spring outgoing.

Qingming Festival is said to commemorate Jie Zitui, a faithful minister of Jin state during the Spring and Autumn Period, who had cut a piece of flesh from his own leg to save his hungry lord. Nineteen years later when the lord decided to reward him for his loyalty, he just refused to take it and secluded himself in a mountain with his mother. To force him to come out, Chonger, the king of Jin State ordered his soldiers to set the mountain on fire. Finally, Jie and his mother were found dead around a willow tree. In order to commemorate Jie, Chonger commanded that the day Jie died be Hanshi (The Cold Food) Festival when only cold food could be eaten. The next year, when Chonger went to the mountain to sacrifice to Jie, he found the willow tree revived, so he ordered that the day after Hanshi Festival was to be Qingming Festival. Gradually the two festivals were incorporated as one.

The main customs of Qingming Festival include tomb sweeping, having a spring outing, and flying kites. However, some customs like wearing willow branches on the head and riding on swings have also brought lots of joys to the people. Generally speaking, it is a mixture of sorrow and happiness.

2) Halloween

Halloween, the shortening form of All Hallows' Evening or All Hallows' Eve, is a festival celebrated on the night of October 31, which is said to be brought to North America by Irish and Scottish immigrants in the 19th century. From late 20th century it begins to be celebrated in some western countries such as the United States, Canada, the United Kingdom as well as Australia and New Zealand and so on.

(1) Origin

The origin of Halloween is the ancient Celtic festival known as Samhain (a time named by the ancient pagans to preserve stock of supplies and prepare for the winter), marking a celebration at the end of the harvest season. Most ancient Gaels hold the belief that the boundary between the living world and the dead overlapped and the decedents would come back to life, causing disasters such as sickness or crop damages on October 31st.

(2) Trick-or-treating

As one of the major traditions of Halloween, Trick-or-treat is an activity for children in which they go from door to door around the neighborhood in costumes, demanding for treats like candies by asking the neighbors "Trick or treat?" Otherwise, they will threat to play a trick on the homeowner or his families if their request is rejected. Therefore, it has become commonly accepted that if a person lives nearby a neighborhood with children, he is supposed to prepare treats in advance for trick-or-treaters.

(3) Halloween Witches

According to various legends, witches have long been related to Halloween, who tend to gather twice a year with the change of the seasons, on April 30, the eve of May Day and the other is on the eve of October 31, Halloween's Eve.

When the witches arrive by broomsticks, they start to celebrate a party hosted by the devil. They love to conduct magical mischief such as casting spells on people or transforming themselves into different forms. It is said that people deliberately wear the clothes on wrong side out and walk backwards on Halloween night in order to meet the witch, which has become the origin for young people to dress up in ghost costumes when Halloween comes in the western countries.

6.2.4 Festival Taboos

Both in China and western countries there are some taboos in celebrating festivals. In China, on Spring Festival, it is prohibited to say "完了"(over), "没了"(no more) and so on; people try to avoid breaking any utensil, and if broken, the person must say "岁岁平安"(be safe and sound every year). On the first day of the first lunar month, it is a taboo to sweep the trash because in most Chinese's eyes it will take their good fortune away.

In some western countries, when Christmas is coming, people make puddings for each member of the family and make a wish by stirring them. People should stir the pudding clockwisely instead of doing it counterclockwisely and they mustn't tell their wish to anyone, otherwise, their wish will not take an effect. On New Year's Day, the westerners think that the first visitor will determine the coming year's fortune, therefore, they hope that the first visitor is a young man with black hair rather than the one with red hair and cross eyes. Sometimes they will invite a young male friend as the first visitor in advance.

6.3 Customs and Ceremonies of Baby's Birth

Having a new baby is definitely a big thing. Different regions have different cultural traditions about the new birth in the world. From the pregnancy period to the new baby's birth, there are many different kinds of rituals or ceremonies implying deep cultural meanings. A new child brings lots of hope and joy not only to the parents, but also to the family and even the society. Therefore, people from different cultures tend to hold various ceremonies to celebrate the birth of a new baby.

6.3.1 Customs of Baby's Birth in China

In China, the birth of a new life in a family has been endowed with a special significance to the community, and a number of birth rituals are often connected with praying blessing for a new born baby as well as driving evil spirits away from the mother. Consequently, the birth of a new life is usually associated with the following customary rituals.

1) Three Mornings

Three mornings refers to the birth ceremony held on the third morning after a baby was born. Parents tend to send red eggs with the even number for a girl and the odd number for a boy to their close family and friends. Sometimes they may send a few boxes of fruits. Returning gifts might include two kinds of cake, brown sugar, millet, eggs, and walnut meats.

2) First Month Confinement

For Chinese women, it is common for them to stay on the bed for one month after the delivery, which is usually called "sitting the month" in most places since the first month is regarded to be very important to a new mother. During the month, the mother needn't do any housework but simply lie in bed to rest and feed the infant, which is beneficial to her recuperation. Certain foods, such as boiled pig's trotters, the millet porridge and the boiled eggs are encouraged to be eaten, which are believed to help the mother regain her strength, reducing the time of her recovery. Furthermore, she is forbidden to take a bath within the month in case the "wind" or the cold will enter the internal body, resulting lifelong harm to the mother's physical health.

3) First Month Celebration

Most Chinese people regard the completion of the full 30 days as a mile-stone for the new-born baby. Therefore, when a baby is one month old, they prefer to celebrate his or her 30th day for the baby's birth (*Manyue*).

At the moment, most families will worship Buddha, Dao and some other deities by burning incenses, offering many kinds of food to inform the ancestors about the coming of the new family member and praying for the healthy growth of the child.

The gifts for *Manyue* celebration vary regionally but red eggs are essential as a symbol of fertility. Other typical foods include cakes, chicken, savory glutinous rice and pig trotters. Before the dinner, the guests will present their gifts to the newborn baby including gold bangles, chains and usually money in red packets. Gold jewelry is a popular gift among grandparents as the most highly prized metal for the Chinese.

In the modern society, *Manyue* celebration is always held in the restaurants by inviting the guests to a dinner. In Guangdong province, the restaurants prepare the red eggs and pickled ginger for the guests ahead of time. Pickled ginger is preferable because the Cantonese word for sour shares the similar pronunciation as the word for grandson, with families hoping for the arrival of more grandsons (Zhang Liyu & Chen Luoyu, 2016).

6.3.2 Customs of Baby's Birth in Western Countries

Compared to Chinese birth customs, "Baptism" and "First Communion" are very popular in the western countries.

1) Baptism

Baptism has existed in the West for thousands of years. It is believed that a women should make use of the rituals for pregnancy and birth as the opportunity to fulfill her dual responsibilities: a mother at home and a woman in the society. In this case, baptism will be favorable to help build up the baby's new image in the community.

The ceremony of baptism is usually held in a church. The parents, godparents, relatives and friends will be present. In the procedure, the priest usually asks them, "Do you believe and trust in God, the father who has made Heaven and Earth?", "Do you believe and trust in his Son Jesus Christ who has redeemed the mankind?" and "Do you believe and trust in his Holy Spirit who has given life to the people of God?" Hearing each of these three questions, they must answer "I believe and trust in Him".

Baptism is a sacrament of admission to the Christian church. For those Christians, Baptism is not a form but a ritual, signifying their identification with Christ.

2) First Communion

For most Westerners, "First Communion" is also an important event during a baby's

growth. The western parents believe if their babies are religious they might benefit from belonging to a church. The baby will have a sense of belonging and getting some moral and ethical guidance from the church. And as Catholicism, the parents pay great attention to the first communion of their babies.

6.4 Different Birthday Celebrations

It was said that people never celebrated birthdays in ancient period because there was no method to mark time. Only after they observed the moon's cycle and the change of four seasons, did they begin to have the sense of time, which was considered to be the origin of birthday celebration.

6.4.1 Chinese Birthday Celebration

1) First Birthday Celebration

For most Chinese, a baby's first birthday is a very important event to a family, which can be celebrated according to either the lunar calendar or the solar calendar. Usually, the parents will prepare a big banquet for friends and relatives.

Zhuazhou or "Grabbing Test on the baby's first birthday" is the most interesting and important traditional custom, which can be dated back to the period of Three Kingdoms in the history. Nowadays it is still a popular custom in many places in China. When the baby's first birthday comes, it is common that his future is expected to be foretold by taking the item with his hands. During the ceremony, parents tend to place a bunch of items in front of the baby, who will choose randomly from them. What the baby has chosen is said to reveal his or her future character and the career preference.

The items for baby to choose from possess different symbolic meanings: a Chinese brush pen, ink, paper, or an ink stone all stand for a future scholar; an abacus means a future businessman and coins signify a future blessed with fortune. With the progress of times, an abacus is replaced by a calculator and coins by cash or credit cards.

Decent gifts for this occasion again include cash in a red envelop as a symbol for good luck; toys or clothing with embroidered tigers which are believed to be guardians of safety in Chinese culture; eggs which are also dyed red for more good blessings.

To summarize, parents and relatives put their substantial hope on the future of their babies, using such a custom as a way of expressing their good wishes.

2) Other Birthday Celebrations

Traditionally, as far as most Chinese are concerned, only a few birthdays are important, namely the 1st, 10th, 60th, 70th and 80th birthday. The reason why the seniors and the babies receive particular consideration is that in Chinese culture, the elderly are honored with great respect and it's a family's responsibility to preserve the bloodline and ensure the inheritance of the following generations (Zhang Liyu & Chen Luoyu, 2016).

In particular, a 60th birthday is the occasion when the astrological cycle of 12 animals and the five elements of wood, fire, earth, metal and water come together, making it a significant celebration in Chinese culture. Gifts for Chinese elders are usually articles that symbolize longevity, including old miniature trees, wine, packages of long noodles and homemade peaches (which aren't really peaches, but steamed bun shaped like peaches) and money in red envelopes. These items are usually given at even numbers. Chinese never send a clock as a birthday gift to the seniors, since its pronunciation resembles the pronunciation of the Chinese character "终" which means the end of life.

In addition to the above mentioned occasions, annual solar or lunar birthdays are supposed to be enjoyed by having long noodles, which indicates the longevity. They must be prepared without being cut or made with every effort not to bite them short. However, with the influence of the western culture, not many Chinese celebrate birthdays in the traditional way, especially among the youngsters. Instead, they observe annual birthday by arranging a gathering and sharing a birthday cake with the participants.

6.4.2 Western Birthday Celebration

Generally speaking, there are a number of varied customs associating with the birthday celebration in the western countries.

1) Birthday Cakes and Candles

The history of cakes and candles dates back to Ancient Greece, when round cakes were

made to honor Artemis, the lunar goddess, with a couple of candles lit to symbolize the glow of the moon. Little by little, people from other cultures began to follow the customs. And instead of being merely taken as a sacrifice, the cake could also be eaten, thus becoming the common food.

2) Birthday Cards

The exchange of greeting cards has existed in the western culture since early times.

The oldest card was believed to be created in England in the 1400s, but the tradition of sending birthday cards took hold until the mid-1800s. Before that, birthday celebration was a luxury for wealthy families. By the middle of the century, with the stamps being used, the delivery of personal greetings turned much easier, and the printing processes became less costly, making the cards affordable to common families and later they became more and more popular both in Europe and America.

With the technological progress, birthday cards have become more and more attractive and colorful with the appearance of many different types. One change is the application of music, namely "audio cards", which often contains parts of music. Another improvement is the use of voice recording technology, adding a personalized voice message for the birthday card recipient. Nowadays the e-card has become more and more popular and taken place of a physical card.

3) Birthday Parties

In the ancient times, many superstitious beliefs were related to one's birthday. For instance, both the Greek and Roman cultures held that every person owned a protective spirit who protected him in life, particularly on the birthday. Another belief was that birthdays were the occasions where individuals were more vulnerable to be harmed easily by evil spirits. On that day, to keep the bad spirits away, the birthday person would be surrounded by friends and family members with gifts as well as good wishes, which is the origin of birthday parties.

As time goes by, birthdays have developed from simple celebration with typical presents and good wishes to a significant annual event. Nowadays most people prefer to hold a birthday party especially for their children on some important occasions such as the transition from the childhood to the adulthood. Examples of such parties include the sweet sixteenth party in North American and the quinceanera(成人礼) in Latin American.

Western birthday parties usually contain some common rituals. The guests are supposed to bring some gifts to attend the party. The surroundings are often decorated with colorful ornaments, such as balloons and banners. Before having the birthday cake, some candles on it will be lit, with all the guests singing "Happy Birthday to You". After making a wish and blowing out all the candles, the honored person will cut the cake and have it distributed among the guests. At parties for children, in particular, there is time reserved for the "gift opening" when the birthday kid unpacks each of the gifts in front of all the guests. On this occasion, it is also common for the host to give rewarding gifts to the attendees which are called "goodie bags".

6.5 Different Grown-up Ceremony for Children

Besides birth customs and birthday party, there are some other things worth discussing in Chinese and western cultures. They are "Grown-up Ceremony" and "Western Proms".

6.5.1 Chinese Grown-up Ceremony

The traditional Chinese Grown-up Ceremony dates back to Zhou Dynasty, which has experienced a gradual evolving process. In the traditional Chinese culture, the main purpose of holding an adult ceremony is to make the ceremony receiver conscious of the responsibility on the shoulders, taking the young man into the adult society. As the *Book of Rites* records, males used to receive a capping ceremony at 20 while a hairpin ceremony used to be held for females at 15. Both capping and hairpin ceremonies are traditional adult rituals in the ancient China.

Traditionally, after the completion of the grown-up ceremony, young men are granted adult clothes. It is time for them to stop behaving like a child and take the responsibility as an adult in order to maintain their dignity and achieve the moral excellence. Nowadays, the grown-up ceremony is usually held in the last year of the senior high school before the young take part in the college entrance examination to reinforce their sense of social responsibility.

6.5.2 Western Grown-up Ceremonies

The Grown-up Ceremony is also held in western countries. In Australia, New Zealand

and the United Kingdom, young men tend to celebrate it at either 18 or 21. Eighteenth or twenty-first birthday celebrations typically take the form of an extravagant party with some more valuable gifts from their guests and friends. Drinking plays an important role in the 18th birthday ceremony, as it is the age when one can legally purchase and drink alcohol. So, lots of champagne will be served on the celebrations. As a result, many 18th birthdays are celebrated by holding a large party with friends around. Despite 18 being the legal age of adulthood, most young men do not immediately take on the role of adults, such as moving out of home or gaining full-time employment, instead, studying or working as an apprentice is still a common phenomenon. In New Zealand and Australia when the young man is twenty-one years old, it is a custom for family members to assemble his photos, videos in his or her childhood to display at a celebration or for a good friend to make a celebrating speech.

In America, for most high school students, holding a romantic and big prom will be one of their unforgettable experiences. Both boys and girls pay more attention to such a prom than the graduation examination, because the test can be held for another time, but it is unlikely to have high school prom for the second time.

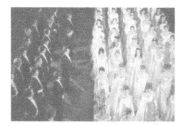

Generally, the organizers tend to prepare for the school prom a few months in advance. People will dress them up to take part in the prom. For girls, they usually spend several days picking up the evening dress as well as the shoes to match, with high-end salon hair, nails and some glittering ornaments. Boys often wear casual and costly tuxedo, with lots of hair waxes and colognes. The school prom is not celebrated in the school auditorium; instead it is often held in some advanced hotels or clubs. But nowadays, more and more students choose gardens, beaches or forests as the celebrating places for school proms.

In general, boys and girls tend to find their own partners before the prom. They can choose their good friends or classmates as their dance partners, but no rules require the students to find a partner to attend. However if a boy wants to have a partner, he needs to inform her/him in advance.

Chapter 6 Social Customs and Etiquette

6.6 Different Rituals of Marriage

Marriage is one of the most important events in a person's life, marking a new turning point of one's life, which means a union or a legal contact between the young couple with their respective rights and obligations. Therefore, learning about the marriage in different cultures will help to recognize about their different customs further and avoid unnecessary misunderstandings.

6.6.1 Chinese Marriage Customs

1) Traditional Chinese Marriage Customs

The conventional marriage rituals, as a reflection of the traditional Chinese culture, vary greatly from region to region over the time. However, though the rituals change with time, the traditional Chinese marriage customs basically remain, known as "Three Letters and Six Etiquettes".

(1) Three Letters

Three Letters refers to the betrothal letter, the gift letter and the wedding letter, each of which is used in a different period of the marriage.

—Betrothal Letter: an official contract of a marriage between the two families;

—Gift Letter: a letter with a list clearly defining the kinds and quantities of the attached gifts;

—Wedding Letter: an official letter welcoming the bride to the bridegroom's home.

(2) Six Etiquettes(六礼)

Six Etiquettes has been passed down as the traditional Chinese marriage customs since the Western Zhou Dynasty, representing the significance that goddess attaches to marriage which is somehow viewed as superstition from modern perspectives.

—Proposing Marriage (*Nacai*): The boy's parents ask a go-between to propose to a potential girl at the girl's home.

—Matching Birthdates (*Wenming*): After a smooth proposal, the match-maker tends to inquire about the four pillars of birth time (referring to the year, month, day and hour of birth respectively), known as *Bazi* in Chinese astrology of the couple-to-be and present it to a fortune-teller to see whether the couple will match in the future. Only if the result is positive, can the marriage ritual continue.

—Submitting Betrothal Gifts (*Naji*): Once the birth-dates of the couple-to-be are proved to be matchable, the boy's parents will arrange and submit betrothal gifts to the girl's family, including the betrothal letter.

—Presenting Wedding Gifts (*Nazheng*): Should the betrothal gifts be accepted, the boy's parents would send wedding gifts to the girl's family. The wedding gifts usually include money, jewelry, cakes and sacrificial articles.

—Selecting a Wedding Date (*Qingqi*): The boy's parents choose a wedding date according to the divination and the solicited agreement of the girl's parents. Once the date is fixed, the girl's party will present the bride's dowry to the bridegroom's house before the wedding day.

The traditional dowry comprises jewelry, scissors (symbol of the inseparable future), a ruler (symbol of rich property), sugar (symbol of the happy marriage), a silver purse (symbol of fortune), a vase (symbol of wealth and honor), quilts, pillows, and clothes (symbol of many offsprings).

—Holding a Wedding Ceremony (*Qinying*)

(3) Marriage Ceremonies

It has been customary for the bridegroom to welcome the bride at her home and carry her to his home in a bride's sedan since the Western Zhou Dynasty. The wedding ceremony is usually held at the boy's house, after which he will take her as his wife.

On the morning of the wedding, a respectable old woman will help the bride to tie up her hair with colorful cotton threads. Red is the popular color in the Chinese traditional wedding because it indicates the fortune and happiness in the young couple's future life. When the bridegroom arrives, the bride who is covered by a red handkerchief usually cries in the face of her family members, showing her reluctance to leave home. Then, her elder brother will lead her to the sedan.

Generally the groom will encounters a series of difficulties intentionally set on his path before he is allowed to see his future wife.

Upon the arrival of the sedan at the groom's residence, there will be music and firecrackers to create a merry atmosphere. The couple will be led along the red carpet, kowtowing three times to worship the heaven, their parents and their mates. Then the new couple will go to their bridal chamber, and the guests will be treated with a feast. On the night of the wedding day, there is a custom in some places that the relatives or the friends are supposed to banter the newlyweds to bring noisiness and scare off the evil spirits deliberately.

On the third day of the marriage, the new couple will return to the bride's home to see her parents, having a dinner with all her relatives.

Admittedly, marriage convention differs from region to region, and some major etiquettes have been maintained for thousands of years. However, most people have tended to abandon some of them and advocate simplified procedures since the founding of modern China.

2) Contemporary Chinese Marriage Customs

In the past century, China has undergone dramatic social, economic and cultural changes. Accordingly, the contemporary Chinese marriage customs pay more attention to the fact of the marriage rather than its process. Therefore, the procedures of the wedding rituals have been simplified greatly, and the wedding banquet has become the core of the whole ceremony.

(1) Marriage Certificate

With the foundation of the People's Republic of China, the Chinese marriage system has gone through a complete change; the first marriage law issued in 1950 has abolished the feudalistic factors of the traditional marriage, stipulating the principles of the freedom and the monogamy in marriage.

When two young persons decide to get married, they have to register at the local government agency, applying for the marriage certificate so as to become a legitimate couple.

Though the wedding certificate represents the legal status for the marriage, the young couple can be publicly regarded as the married ones only after the completion of their wedding ceremony in contemporary China.

(2) Wedding Photos

The practice of wedding photos originates from taking a group photo on the occasion of marriage in 1920s when it became a fashion for the young couples to take pictures in wedding garments. In 1960s, the traditional mandarin cheongsam and Western wedding gown were replaced by casual clothes in people's wedding photos. Since 1990s, it has become a popular tendency for the young couples to take the wedding photos in the professional photograph studios, which now has become a necessity for young couples.

The enlarged wedding photos are usually hung up in the newly-weds' bedroom, reminding them of their happy moments which deserve to be shared with others.

(3) Bridal Cars

For most young couples, bridal cars are indispensable in the wedding. Since the 1930s, the bridal sedan has been gradually replaced by automobiles which are decorated with bunches of fresh flowers to maintain some traditional elements. And usually, the more luxurious the cars are, the more dignity the couple has won as a reflection of their families' wealth or status.

(4) Wedding Banquet

In modern China, the wedding banquet is the most important procedure in the whole wedding ceremony. The formal marriage banquet usually serves the guest with more than 12 courses. All the guests are seated at the round tables, following the carefully-arranged seating chart to ensure that everybody can take their seats with their acquaintances after presenting the red envelop with cash in it as the gift.

Before the feast starts, some guests may take pictures with the bride and groom. During the banquet, the bride and groom tend to go from table to table to toast the guests with the companion of their parents or their best friends sometimes. The guests also toast the young couple.

Meanwhile, the friends often play pranks on the newly-weds with the intention of creating a merry atmosphere, making the groom publicly show his love and care to the bride. And the bride tends to wear several different gowns during the whole wedding ceremony alternately.

In the end, the newlyweds and their relatives stand at the door, expressing their thanks to the guests for attending the wedding.

6.6.2 Western Marriage Customs

1) Engagement

In western culture, engagement rings are constantly associated with marriage; while being particularly worn by the woman, it can be regarded as a symbol of making a silent declaration of her betrothal. The concept of using the ring is closely related with its shape. In Ancient Egypt, the ring also symbolizes the sacred moon and sun gods, with the circular shape representing an eternal bond. Meanwhile, the hole in the center of the ring implies a doorway into the unknown world. Nowadays, some wedding rings are designed in two halves. The woman wears one half as an engagement ring and then the other half is to be worn after getting married.

The engagement ring is worn on the fourth finger of the left hand in the United States, the United Kingdom, Ireland, Canada, and Australia. People from Continental Europe and some other countries wear it on the other hand instead. The reason why the fourth is the ring finger concerns the vena amorism, the "vein of love" in Latin, which supposedly runs in a direct line from the ring finger to the heart.

2) Marriage Customs

(1) Bachelor Party

Bachelor party, the celebration in the groom's honor which used to be called the bachelor dinner, or the stag party, is the marriage custom that has existed for more than one thousand and five hundred years. Firstly the activity appeared in Sparta in the fifth century, as an occasion for military soldiers to feast and toast on the eve of a friend's wedding. Nowadays, a bachelor party usually takes place closely prior to the actual wedding as the time for the groom to have the last taste of freedom. Although viewed as raucous, bachelor party is originally conducted to allow the groom and his wedding attendants to relieve themselves from the great nervousness before the important day.

(2) Bridal Showers

The origin of bridal showers comes from Holland. If a bride's father does not favor the husband-to-be, he usually shows his disagreement by not providing her with the necessary dowry. Therefore, the bride's friends tend to support her by "showering" her with gifts so she will raise enough dowries to marry the man of her choice. While the customs of dowries are long gone today, the practice of presenting gifts to the bride-to-be survives, becoming popular with the western weddings.

(3) White Weddings

The custom of wearing white could be attributed to Queen Victoria who broke the convention and wore a white wedding dress on the royal wedding. Before that, white was not considered suitable for a royal wedding, but Victoria popularized the white gowns in it and white caught on its popularity ever since. After Victoria's wedding, gold dresses or gold threaded dresses gained popularity among the royals while other brides tended to wear white or pastel dresses, as a way to reflect their social status.

Up to the mid-twentieth century, many brides in the United Kingdom would rather wear a special dress such as an evening dress rather than a traditional or gown-type wedding dress. In America, it is the same case that most practical brides prefer a formal dress that can be worn on other occasions.

A western white wedding is usually conducted in a church. Some churches require that the couples should join parish or pledge to do so after marriage. The white wedding in the United States can also be held at home, a private club or somewhere like a garden, etc.

(4) Wedding Reception

At the wedding reception, the bride and groom tend to show their gratitude to their guests by cutting the wedding cake and sharing it with all the guests as well as friends around. The guests usually interact with each other happily while enjoying cakes, punch and other treats. Another interesting activity is the bride's throwing her bouquet to the single girls and the girl who catches the bouquet will become the next one to marry. During the reception, playful friends often decorate the couple's car with tissue paper, tin cans or a sign of "Just Married". Once the reception is over, the newlyweds run to their car and speed off. Many couples prefer to lighten the candle, which is thought to be an evolution from the use of fire mentioned above with the intention to protect their life together from the spirits.

Exercises

I. **Questions for Discussion**

1. Why do most Chinese parents pay great attention to their children's first birthday? Can what the baby grabs on the first birthday determines his or her future career in your opinion? Why or why not?

2. Do you think it is necessary to hold the grown-up ceremony for the children when they are eighteen years old? Why do you think so? Can you tell something about your own grown-up ceremony?

3. As a young generation, is it wise for all of us to follow our parents' words while choosing our future spouse? Why or why not? And which do you prefer, the Chinese

marriage or the western marriage? Please give your reason.

4. Can you share your opinion on more and more young Chinese show great passion on western "festivals"?

5. There's a drastic change in Chinese wedding customs, what do you think would be the reasons for this change?

Ⅱ. Comprehension Check

Decide whether the following statements are true (T) or false (F).

_____ 1. For Chinese women, it is common for them to stay on the bed for three months after the delivery since the first three months are regarded to be very important to a new mother, which is usually called "sitting the month" in most places.

_____ 2. The western parents pay great attention to their children's first communion, because they believe if their children are religious they might benefit from belonging to a church.

_____ 3. The history of cakes and candles dates back to Ancient Great Britain, when round cakes were made to honor Queen Elizabeth, with a couple of candles lit to symbolize her love.

_____ 4. In the ancient China, males used to receive a capping ceremony at 18 while a hairpin ceremony used to be held for females at 16.

_____ 5. In Australia, New Zealand and the United Kingdom, the young men tend to celebrate Groun-up ceremonies at either 18 or 21.

_____ 6. In China, *Three Letters* refers to the betrothal letter, the gift letter and the wedding letter, each of which is used in a different period of the marriage.

_____ 7. The custom of wearing white could be attributed to Queen Elizabeth who granted the law and ordered all the royal members to wear a white wedding dress.

_____ 8. In China, on the night of the wedding day, a custom in some places is that the relatives or friends are supposed to banter the newlyweds to bring noisiness and scare off the evil spirits deliberately.

_____ 9. The engagement ring is worn on the fourth finger of the left hand in most European countries and North American countries.

_____ 10. During the Spring Festival, pasting the "Fu" upside down, which stands for the arrival of happiness, is very popular with most families in China.

Ⅲ. **Vocabulary**

Complete the following sentences with the words given below and each word can be used only once.

| beneficial | legally | inheritance | lifelong | milestone |
| foretold | popular | commemorate | reluctance | gratitude |

1. During the first month after the baby's birth, the mother needn't do any housework but simply lie in bed to rest and feed the infant, which is _____ to her recuperation in most Chinese' opinion.
2. In China, during the first month confinement the mother is usually forbidden to take a bath within the month in case the "wind" or the cold will enter the internal body, resulting in the _____ harm to the mother's physical health.
3. Most Chinese people regard the completion of the full 30 days as a _____ for the baby.
4. In China when a baby's first birthday comes, it is common that his future is expected to be _____ by taking the item with his hands.
5. Compared with Chinese birth customs, "Baptism" and "First Communion" are very _____ in the western countries.
6. The reason why the seniors and the babies receive particular consideration is that in Chinese culture, the elderly are honored with great respect and it's a family's responsibility to preserve the bloodline and ensure the _____ of the following generations.
7. Drinking plays an important role in the western eighteenth birthday ceremony, as it is the age where one can _____ purchase and drink alcohol.
8. Qingming Festival is said to _____ Jie Zitui, a faithful minister of Jin state in the Spring and Autumn Period.
9. When the bridegroom arrives, the bride, covered by a red handkerchief, usually cries in the face of her family members, showing her _____ to leave home on the Chinese wedding day.
10. At the wedding reception, the bride and groom tend to show their _____ to their guests by cutting the wedding cake and sharing all the guests and friends around.

Ⅳ. Translation

Translate the following Chinese phrases into English and vice versa.

1. 做满月
2. 婴儿洗礼
3. 抓周
4. 成人礼
5. 婚宴
6. First Communion
7. birthday candles
8. Proposing Marriage
9. Family Reunion Dinner
10. Bachelor Party

Ⅴ. Case Analysis

Case 1

Bart Rapson had brought his family to the Philippines to a job assignment for a multinational corporation. While not particularly religious themselves, having largely abandoned the practice of Catholicism except for token appearance at Christmas and Easter, they still felt that their children might benefit from belonging to a church. They explained to friends that the church could give children a sense of belonging and provide some moral and ethical guidance. Since Philippines believe in Catholic largely, it was easy for Bart to place his 7-year-old daughter in a Sunday school class that would prepare her for her First Communion. As the day approached, Bart planned for another church party, inviting colleagues and their families from work. One Filipino colleague, Manuel, to whom Bart felt especially close, kept putting off an answer to Bart's invitation, saying neither "yes" nor "no". Finally Bart said, "My wife needs to know how many people to cook for." Still not giving a yes or no answer, Manuel later called and said that he would be attending a different party that would be attended by other Filipinos, but Bart did not recognize anyone from the list. Manuel said that he would try to stop by sometime during Bart's party.

Bart was quite upset. He complained, "If this is supposedly a Catholic country, why would they not place a value on this? Why would he turn down a once-in-lifetime gathering, my daughter's First Communion, to go to a party with friends he admits to seeing all the time?" After the party, Bart was merely cordial to Manuel—there were no longer any indications of friendliness. Manuel was puzzled, and had no idea what the problem was. The director of the organization, a sensitive person, picked up the cause and realized that there was a strained relationship.

Questions for discussion:

Why did Bart feel upset in this case? What was Manuel's problem and what should he pay attention to next time?

Case 2

Mark and Jane are the young couples who come from America, and they have worked in an international corporation situated in Shanghai for five years. Wang Wei and Zhu Dan are their classmates in America and they work in the same company now. Last month, Wang Wei and Zhu Dan held their wedding ceremony which they looked forward to for a long time in the most famous restaurant of Shanghai—Heping Restaurant. As their classmates and their best friends, Mark and Jane decided to attend their best friends' wedding, giving their best wishes to them at the wedding. On the wedding Day, the American young couple came to the wedding location earlier with their wedding gifts, a beautiful album and a bundle of pink lily.

When seeing their American best friends' coming, Wang Wei and Zhu Dan felt very happy. However, when they saw the gift taken by their friends, they felt disappointed in their mind. During the whole wedding ceremony, the young couple greeted warmly to all the guests with smile on their face. And Mark and Jane also felt very cheerful because it was the first time to attend such a fervent wedding in China. After the wedding, Mark and Jane found the change of the newly-wed's attitudes towards them and they couldn't feel the warmth and friendliness from their best friends any longer. Both Mark and Jane were very confused about what had happened to them and they had no idea what they should do to make up the relationship with their best friends in China.

Questions for discussion:

What led to the change of Wang Wei and Zhu Dan's attitudes towards their American friends? What advice can you give to the young American couples?

VI. Activities

Surf the Internet and collect enough information, compare the social customs from the following aspects between China and the Western countries and make a presentation in front of class.

1. Food and Drink
2. Clothing

3. Architecture
4. Table Etiquette
5. Social Communicative Ritual
6. Birth Ceremony
7. Birthday Celebration
8. Marriage Customs
9. Marriage and Family Sense
10. Other Festivals Comparison

Ⅶ. **Video Watching**

Four Weddings and a Funeral《四个婚礼和一个葬礼》

Chapter 7   International Business Etiquette

Etiquette reflects our cultural norms, generally accepted ethical codes, and the rules of various groups we belong to. It governs good behaviours, our social and business interactions and evolves to match the times.

However, sometimes what is considered good etiquette in one country may be considered extremely bad manners in another country. A better understanding of international communication etiquette is of great help to develop good business relationship overseas.

7.1　Introduction

7.1.1　Business Etiquette

Business etiquette is the set of rules by which one conducts business. As Susie Wilson, a famous Australian etiquette expert puts it: "Generally, business etiquette is a behaviour standard and activity programs when people do business with others in business world, including two aspects: etiquette and ceremony." (Susie W., 2014) In business interactions, etiquette facilitates a professional standard of conduct that each business has in common with the other businesses.

Business etiquette is not just knowing what to discuss during a business dinner or how to address colleagues; it is a way of presenting yourself that you will be taken seriously. This involves demonstrating that you have the self-control necessary to be good at your job, expressing a knowledge of business situations and having the ability to make others comfortable around you. Proper etiquette sets a tone for clients and customers that the business has a productive and successful environment. It will help build strong relationships with business partners, promote positive atmosphere in workplace, and prevent misunderstanding as well. Poor business etiquette will cost you the trust of your workers and your customers, and the loss of valuable business opportunities.

7.1.2 International Business Etiquette

Each culture has its own etiquette rules, many of them unwritten. Business dinner etiquette, dress etiquette, gift-giving etiquette and so on vary greatly between countries and cultures. International business etiquette refers to the habitual form and behaviour which are shaped in people's long-term business activities in the international business and it is the behavior guidance applicable throughout the world. Knowing how to behave in a variety of business situations will help build productive business relationship. Otherwise, it would be hard for intercultural business people to establish harmonious relationship in the global working environment.

Nowadays, more and more multinational companies are founded, thus international business communication becomes an important part in company's routine work. Whoever is going to work in international environment should be aware of the importance of international business etiquette.

7.2 General International Business Etiquette

7.2.1 Greeting

Standard business etiquette establishes generally agreed-upon principles for greetings. Most business greetings begin with a simple and firm handshake, but many countries have their own style of greeting.

For example, in Japan, bowing is considered an appropriate greeting form, although foreigners may be permitted to substitute with a nod of the head. Shaking hands is the most popular greeting in China. Though handshaking starts to be popular in India and Thailand, still the traditional approach in these countries is placing the hands together at chest-level, prayer-like, and bowing. When visiting Asia or the Middle East keep in mind that the customary grip should be gentler and too firm handshake can be defined as aggressive. In Islamic cultures, it is common for Muslim men to shake hands with each other when greeting and say "As-Salam-u-Alaikum" ("Peace be unto you"). While there is debate on the appropriateness of female Muslims shaking hands with men, you should not do so unless the female Muslims initiate the contact. Even you are greeting a male Muslim, you should not reach for his hand unless he initiates the contact.

Hugs and kisses are not considered proper business etiquette for greeting. There is nothing more off-putting(令人厌恶的) than trying to kiss someone who is only expecting a handshake, or holding out your hand pointlessly while the other person bows. Even most Americans and British prefer a firm handshake at the first greeting. Hugging is reserved for close family members and friends. Kissing people when greeting is so intimate an affair that it's usually done only in the context of relatives, lovers, and friends.

Some guidelines for business etiquette greeting may work well in most situations, but some particular customs in some countries should never be neglected. Instead, they should be paid more attention to. If you visit a country for the first time it might be a good idea to find out what is the expected way of greeting there.

7.2.2 Business Card Exchanging

Since business cards play a vital role in almost all business contacts, an important aspect of business protocol(礼仪) is to know the proper procedure for exchanging business cards. In some cultures, the act of exchanging business cards has to be accompanied with protocol. Otherwise, a big offense would be committed to your partner without your awareness in intercultural business. So before you leave for your intercultural affairs, make sure you know the proper way to slip someone your business card.

It is important to include your position and titles or degrees in addition to your company name on your card. In China and Japan, for instance, business cards have to be offered with both hands and you are expected to study them for several seconds and never slip them in your pocket while in the giver's presence. If you have printed your card in Chinese or Japanese as well as English, then present your card with the other person's native language facing up. In the Middle East, however, you are not allowed to use your left hand when offering a business card.

7.2.3 Dressing

Good business etiquette also necessitates dressing appropriately. Buck Rodgers, author of *The IBM Way*, holds that the way you dress affects the way you are perceived, and the way you are perceived, is the way you are treated. Wearing the appropriate clothing will earn you a good first impression and set the tone for how you will be seen. The importance of dressing in business world would never be overestimated.

There are many variables to be taken into consideration when choosing the perfect outfit for a special occasion in western countries. You can make full use of the clues you are given on the invitation, or by the nature of the event.

Firstly, the words on the invitation will give some clues. Sometimes there are some indications of a dress code on the invitation letter. Deciphering the notation at the bottom of the invitation shoule be taken into consideration. "Black Tie" literally refers to the dress for the males in attendance. "Cocktail", for example, calls for "an elegant-looking dress in any color, but no formal gowns". "White Tie" affairs "are the most formal of all functions". A woman should wear a long, formal dress, while her male companion should be in "Full Dress", which means a black tailcoat, black pants, and a shirt, tie and vest which are all white.

Secondly, the time and location indicated on the invitation will also give clues. A beach or outdoor wedding means that you must take the location into consideration. A "brunch" reception or "afternoon tea" calls for an outfit that is quite different from a "cocktail reception".

The dress etiquette for business women in Western countries is somewhat more complex. They should always opt for conventional and modest business attire. Women should wear a suit or dress with jacket in major cities. Wearing classic clothing and classic colors of navy, gray, ivory, and white will ensure you a confident and conservative appearance. What might be appropriate for the evening might be totally inappropriate for the daytime. Ladies would find acceptance when wearing a plunging neckline in the evening social event, but would be scandalously clad in the same gown during the day. Wearing a low-cut, off-the-shoulder gown for the day's social event may be a much wrong dress etiquette. Some more tips for ladies' clock clothing are provided by some how-to books that ladies are not to show their ankles except in an unusual circumstance of some description. A lady would be considered vulgar indeed if she lifts both sides of her skirts, even when making her way up or down a staircase, or stepping up onto or down from a curb. It is only acceptable when crossing a muddy spot.

In China, on business occasion, in medium dark-colored, conservative suits with shirts and ties would be an appropriate look for men. Conservative business suits or dresses and blouses are appropriate for women. Avoid low necklines, high-heels and tight-fitting or sleeveless attire. Jeans and business casual attire are not recommended at the first meeting. In warmer months, slacks and collared shirts are usually acceptable.

Business suit and tie are appropriate for businessmen in most, if not all, cultures. Generally, dark colored business suits in classic colors of gray and navy are appropriate for business negotiation and meeting. For an important formal meeting, a white dress shirt is appropriate. While for a less formal one a light blue shirt will still give you a conservative appearance. In the more conservative countries, long sleeves and long skirts are usually expected. Loose fitted clothes with bare or minimal makeup could even be required.

Always make sure your clothes are clean and wrinkle-free. Good grooming (hair and makeup) is an important part of the overall look for business women, but excessive use of makeup should be avoided.

Appropriate dressing indicates that you take yourself and your job seriously and shows consideration for others as well. An unkempt(头发蓬乱的) appearance indicates that you do not care about yourself or respect those around you.

If you are in any doubt about what is appropriate to wear and what is not always seek local advice about the dress etiquette, and check in advance the dress code for any specific events you will attend, i.e. conferences, formal business dinners, etc.

7.2.4 Business Negotiation

Business negotiations can be a tricky balancing act. Being too pushy will drive business away unintentionally, while being a bit of soft will make you appear to lack confidence and fortitude. The following negotiation etiquettes will help you avoid stepping on toes and keep goals in perspective so you don't overcommit or overpay.

1) Staying Genuine and Respectful

The No.1 rule of etiquette is to keep a respectful attitude toward investors and business contacts. When you negotiate, you're not just selling a product, promoting an idea or marketing your services—you're selling yourself. Express sincere gratitude, stay humble and never beg for financial resources. Make them trust you that not only your products are valuable, but your skills, passions and expertise are worth the investment.

2) Be Patient and Listen

Take time to listen and don't rush the process. If you don't take time to listen to others' viewpoints, goals and intentions, you might make wrong assumptions. Ask questions, such as "What are you hoping to get out of these negotiations" or "How do you think our company can help you meet your goals?" Take time to listen, even if it tests your patience. You'll likely learn something important in the process that could help you finalize a win-win contract.

3) Sticking to Your Bottom Line

Always know your bottom line before entering business negotiations. Otherwise, you'll waste everyone's time if you have to terminate the meeting to rethink your options.

4) Knowing When to Back Down

Be polite and back down if negotiations become heated. Angry words and threats damage the negotiation process and often force business associates to respond defensively. Try to re-establish common ground, review similar goals, and avoid being competitive or argumentative. Keep in mind the main objective of business negotiation is to find solutions that satisfy both parties. If you try your best to approach the negotiations but get nowhere, you'd better prepare to walk away with your head held high.

5) Observing International Business Etiquette

It's important to do some research on cultural norms before engaging in international negotiations if you don't want to risk offending anyone. Most countries have specific guidelines that govern business negotiations. For example, in China, only the senior Chinese negotiator will speak, so the other part needs to appoint one person from their team to do the same. Be clear, concise and well-prepared to earn respect. The following section presents some essential traits of negotiators from several different countries.

(1) American Negotiators

Americans uphold the spirit of "conquering" when they negotiate. They love to retort and do not give in easily. Americans greatly value fundamental policies, and these policies are often formulated well in advance. Sometimes, a sound concept would still be rejected if it violates fundamental policies. Americans also formulate a backup plan just in case the original proposal is not approved. They are good at utilizing the skills of pausing and being silent; however, they lack the ability to tolerate interruptions. At the end of a negotiation, Americans would want to draw a clear conclusion (exchange of contracts). In other words, they believe that a negotiation has officially come to an end once the contracts have been exchanged. Basically, Americans like to solve a problem item by item. There are 9 Rules of Negotiation for Americans: (1) Everything is negotiable. (2) Never pay the "window sticker" price. Don't be easy to get. (3) Start high and nibble like crazy. (4) No free gifts! Use the big "IF". (5) Start slowly and be patient. (6) Use/beware the power of legitimacy. (7) Make small concessions, especially at the end. (8) Keep looking for creative alternatives. (9) Leave your opponent feeling they have done well.

The biggest difference between Americans and the people in other countries in terms of negotiating is that Americans are preoccupied with the articles in a negotiation, whereas the people in other countries focus on the relationship between them and their opponents. A blind spot shared by Americans is that they believe all the people in the world want to be like Americans. They believe that all the markets should be made open. Even if you are negotiating with them on your own turf, they still want to do things their way. If you are on their turf, their lawyers will present you with a host of rules. Americans love conflict and they do not conceal their skill of intimidating others. American negotiators take a strong stance at the beginning and seldom back down. When necessary, they will only concede on important matters when the negotiation process is near its end.

Nevertheless, Americans still prefer quick negotiations; they are not happy with too much socializing or delay.

(2) German Negotiators

Germans are competitive, ambitious and hard bargainers. In German business, a person's word and handshake are considered his/her bond. If a verbal agreement is made in a business meeting, it is generally considered binding.

Business negotiation tends to be analytical and factual. A well-researched speech with lots of graphs, empirical arguments, and statistics is usually preferred. A direct, matter-of-fact approach will be most appreciated.

Business is hierarchical. Decision-making takes place at the highest levels of the company i.e. top down. It is not appropriate to bypass an associate of equal ranking by consulting with his or her superior, even if negotiations take a long time.

Decision-making is often a slow and detailed process. Do not expect significant conclusions to be reached based on spontaneous or unstructured results. Every aspect of the deal you propose will be pored over by many executives. Do not anticipate being able to speed up this process. If Germans feel rushed to complete a business deal, they may perceive this as a lack of commitment and professionalism.

Germans are detail-oriented and want to understand every innuendo before coming to an agreement. Germans have an aversion to divergent opinions, but they will negotiate and debate an issue fervently. Your attention to detail will not go unnoticed by your German counterparts and will highlight your genuine willingness and enthusiasm to do business with them.

Avoiding contradictory statements, such as following a compliment with a complaint will be considered inconsistency, which may cause a German to reject your statements outright.

Jokes, anecdotes, a "hard sell" approach (which may entail insulting a competitor), or spontaneous presentations are generally considered inappropriate. Slang language and colloquialisms should be kept to a minimum or better yet, not used at all. Final decisions are translated into rigorous and comprehensive action steps that will be carried out to the letter. Once a decision is made, it will not be changed.

(3) French Negotiators

When conducting business negotiations with your French counterparts, you need to be aware that you are very likely to come across bureaucratic and centralized decision-making.

In your negotiations, you have to focus on the subject matter of the deal you are discussing and at no point should you bring in other matters such as family, as this will, if anything, reduce your chances of getting what you want and also possibly offend your negotiation partners.

During a business negotiation, be prepared to answer direct and detailed questions. Your persistence and tenacity are likely to be rewarded since the longer the negotiations continue, the higher are your chances of success, since agreements usually take a long time to reach.

Once a decision has been reached between those in the negotiation process, there is a high likelihood that your French partners will have to go through a similar internal process and therefore even if you have signed a contract, there is a chance that they will come back to re-negotiate it as a result of internal negotiation. The better way is that you should always try and seek out the top decision maker in the French organization to speed up your negotiation.

(4) British Negotiators

The vast majority of British companies and organizations are still characterized by a distinct hierarchy. Although their instructions might be formulated as a polite request or even a mere suggestion, British managers are known to be firm, effective and resolute. Their authority as decision maker is not to be questioned.

The British generally prefer working with a group of people they know, they can relate to and with whom they can identify. Meetings are time-consuming and set well in advance. A set agenda is favored by most parties who typically start discussing business after some introductory small talk.

The British are tough and skillful negotiators. Throughout negotiations it is important to remain calm and polite, whereas an informal, humorous tone may sometimes disguise the actual seriousness of an issue discussed.

Most British business people are following a rational and pragmatic approach. Only on rare occasions a commitment is announced right away, while agreements need to be formalized in writing.

(5) Japanese Negotiators

When having a business negotiation with Japanese, you should dress formally for the meeting and display a conservative demeanour; it's not common for Japanese business people to be brash and abrasive. This behaviour can result in a lack of trust and you might not be taken very seriously.

Wait for direction from your host as to where you should sit. Exceptional importance is placed upon seating in meetings and the position is determined by status. Usually, the highest ranking person will sit at the head of the table and the subordinates will sit on both sides of the table. The ranking will decrease the further down the table (away from the head of the table) you get.

Don't take the lead in the meeting when it comes to sitting, drinking or eating. Wait for others to initiate and you can then follow their lead.

It's important to show interest during the meeting and it's acceptable to take notes or repeat participants' ideas to clarify what has been said. This will keep you involved in the dialogue and shows an interest in what's being said.

7.2.5 Business Dining

Social interaction plays an important role in most business relationship, which means that to get well-prepared for business dinners is also very important for a successful business.

1) Planning and Arriving

(1) Planning

Business meal should be planned at least a week in advance. If possible, find out whether your guests like or dislike a certain cuisine. If hosting a group, especially, from different cultures, choose a restaurant with a diverse menu.

Confirm the time and place and repeat the details of the invitation letter in the conversation with your guest(s) and tell your guests what you expect your guests to prepare and bring any pertinent materials. Reconfirming with your guests is a good etiquette. You can call on the morning of a lunch or dinner, but if you've scheduled a breakfast, you should call the day before.

(2) Arriving

The first rule of dining etiquette is arriving on time. Arriving late, even only five minutes will send a clear message of carelessness and thoughtlessness and leave a bad impression.

Appropriate dressing is very important. You can call the restaurant to see if they have a dressing code.

When you arrive at the restaurant earlier and your host hasn't arrived, it is not rush for you to go to the table and wait there. It is suggested that you wait in the lobby or waiting area for him or her. If you are the host, wait for your guest in the lobby. If some of your guests have already arrived, you should wait in the lobby only until the time the reservation is made for. Then proceed to the table and have the maitre d' or waiter escort the late guests in.

2) Table Manners

Good table manners are an important aspect of all intercultural business etiquette. What is considered good table manners, however, varies greatly between countries. Speaking with your mouth full is acceptable in some cultures, while it is considered extremely rude in others.

The following tips for table manners will help avoid conspicuous and embarrassing blunders when in western countries.

Choosing the correct silver tableware from the variety in front of you is not as difficult as it may first appear. Try to remember that start with the knife, fork, or spoon that is farthest from your plate and the knife is never used for any purpose other than cutting food.

There are American style and European or Continental style of using knife and fork. Either style is considered appropriate. In the American style, one cuts the food by holding the knife in the right hand and the fork in the left hand with the fork tines(尖头) piercing the food to secure it on the plate and then pass the fork to the right hand and eat. Fork tines facing up. The difference is your fork remains in your left hand in the Continental style, tines facing down, the knife in your right hand, and simply eat the cut pieces of food by picking them up with your fork still in your left hand. Don't cut large pieces of food, such as steak or chops, into small pieces all at one time. Cut only one or two bites as you eat.

The meal actually begins only ofter everyone has been served and the host or hostess unfolds his or her napkin. The napkin should be placed on your lap, and after each course, it should be used to gently blot your mouth. The host will signal the end of the meal by placing his or her napkin on the table. Once the meal is over, the napkin should be neatly folded and placed on the left side of your plate.

The food is always passed to the right. It is OK to pass to your immediate left if you are the closest to the item requested. The salt and pepper is expected to passed on together.

Smoking is highly prohibited while dining out. Toothpick using is not recommended at table, but in some countries, toothpick can be used if only you cover your mouth with another hand meanwhile. Applying makeup at the table is also a bad manner. If food spills off your plate, you may pick it up with a piece of your silverware and place it on the edge of your plate. Never spit a piece of food into your napkin.

Ignorance of dining taboos will lead to serious offence. Muslims do not drink alcohol or eat any pork product and many avoid shellfish as well. Jews share some of these food taboos. Hindus avoid beef and most of them are strict vegetarians. Buddhists are often strict vegetarians, but many Thailand Buddhists enjoy beef as long as someone else has done the slaughtering for them. Italians only drink cappuccino in the morning before 10 am.

In general, there are some widely accepted table manners that should be remembered when dining:

(1) Chew with your mouth closed;

(2) Don't talk at a loud volume and with your mouth full. If someone talks to you, don't speak until your mouth is empty;

(3) Refrain from burping, coughing, sneezing or blowing nose at table, but if you have to do so, you may request that action be excused by saying "Excuseme";

(4) Never tilt(倾斜) back your chair or slouch while at the table but you can sit in a relaxed and comfortable position;

(5) Always ask the host or hostess to be excused before leaving the table;

(6) Do not stare at others while he or she is eating, which is considered very rude;

(7) Never talk on your phone or text a friend at the table; if an urgent matter arises, ask host or hostess to be excused, and step away from table

(8) Pay enough attention to food taboos in some countries.

3) Business Meal Follow-up Thank-you Notes

Thank-you note is a note sent by the guest to express thanks for the meal and the enjoyable time, providing a confirmation of any decision that has been made as well. The host should also write to tell the guest how nice it was to have a meal with him or her and briefly recap some business details. Maybe a follow-up phone call by either party could be made as a substitute, but the thank-you note has two advantages: it doesn't interrupt the receiver's job, and it is regarded as warmer and more gracious behavior.

7.2.6 Gifting

In some countries giving a gift is considered as a necessary precursor(前导) for building a business relationship, while in others, gift-giving is considered an ostentatious(炫耀的) practice and highly insulting in certain circumstances.

Gifting right is actually the most difficult aspect of international business etiquette. Answering such questions as what to give, when to give, how to give, how to receive, should you open the gift in front of the giver or not and so on will help you to improve gifting etiquette. Every gift sends a message whether you intend it to do so or not. The message doesn't necessarily have anything to do with the cost of the gift. It primarily has to do with how appropriate the gift is. Gifts generally fall into four categories: practical gifts, decorative gifts, durable gifts, and emotional gifts. First you should decide what underlying messages you want to send to the receiver through the gift. Then you can decide which category of gifts can help you convey the messages. The fundamental principle of gift giving is matching the gift with a person's interest, desire and lifestyle.

If you are invited to be a houseguest, presenting the host with an appropriate gift of thanks is appreciated. Common gifts include quality writing instruments, branded whisky, picture books about one's city, region or county and products one's home country is famous for.

There are two basic rules in international business gift-giving: Firstly, the gift you present should be manufactured in your home country and make sure that the gift is not manufactured in a country or region that may cause insult to the recipient. For example, it would be insulting to give a Saudi Arabian a gift manufactured in Israel. Secondly, gifts with company logos should be used as small token only, not as a major sign of appreciation. Even when logos have to be used, they should only be placed on gifts of the highest quality because even the smallest gift represents your company's image and personality. Keep the logo small so that it doesn't look as though the gift is nothing more than a company advertisement.

In business, gift-giving is also a timely manner, so gifts should be given at the right time. In Europe, gifts are given after the agreement is signed. In Japan and most other Asian countries, gifts are given at the end of the meeting. However, North America is not a gift-giving culture and many American negotiators feel uncomfortable if presented with an expensive gift.

Choosing appropriate wrapping is also very important. In Japan, the wrapping of the gift is at least as important as the gift itself. In Japan and the rest of Asia, people present and receive gifts with both hands, except in Thailand where the gifts are handed over with the right hand supported by the left.

In many Asian cultures, particularly in Japan, it is appropriate to politely show reluctance when accepting a gift. In China, a recipient may refuse a gift at the first, second or third offering so as not to appear overly greedy. In many Asian countries, it is considered very impolite to open a gift in the presence of the gift-giver. While in most western countries like United States and Britain, the giver may even request the recipient open it right away. When in doubt, ask the giver if they would like you to open it immediately.

In many countries, it is also polite to give small gifts when meeting someone. Make sure you find out the local customs and avoid giving an overly expensive gift that the other person will feel the need to reciprocate(回报).

Giving gifts and sending follow up thank-you notes to the individuals or organization that looked after you on your business trip is polite and it will be likely to be remembered favorably for a long time and help you to strengthen your business relationship.

7.2.7 E-Mail Etiquette

Digital communication through e-mails prevails in international business nowadays. Good etiquette in business e-mail communication will help make good impression, which will be invaluable to build trust and confidence in mutual relationship. Below are some guidelines of business e-mails we should attach great importance to.

1) Be Sure to Have a Short and Concise SUBJECT

The subject is the window to e-mail and mostly determines whether the e-mail should be opened or not. The subject should be concise and indicate clearly what the topic of e-mail is. Typos, all caps or all small case can lend to the impression that you may be a spammer.

2) Avoiding Large Attachment if not at the Request

A large attachment should be avoided if not at the request. If you need to send a file (or combination of fields) over 5MB in size, it is very considerable for you to ask the recipient firstly if it is OK to send a large file and then confirm they have the same software and version you do and the appropriate time to make sure they are available to download the large file and keep their e-mail flowing.

3) Removing the Irrelevant Parts of the Previous E-mail

Do not just hit reply and start typing. Editing your e-mail and removing the parts of the previous e-mail that no longer apply to your response will be highly appreciated as it is viewed as a respect for the recipient's time because of the clarity of the digital communication. By making the effort to reply point by point you can keep the conversation on the track with fewer misunderstanding.

4) Using Proper Addressing, Greeting and Salutation

For the new contacts, it is safer to show the highest level of courtesy. The proper title will be followed by the whole family name until the new contact states you can call him by the first name. For instance, "Hello, Mr. White, Dear Ms. Jones, Dr. Smith". Most business people do not mind be called by the first name. However, in some hierarchy culture, it would be viewed as a disrespect.

"Hello, Hi, Good Day." "Thank You." "Sincerely, Best Regards." All those intros and signoffs are a staple of professional business communications that should also be used in business e-mail communications. Not doing so could have your messages misinterpreted as demanding or terse. Always include a salutation and signoff that includes your name with every e-mail. Proper capitalization and punctuation are a must! All caps or all small case will leave the e-mail receiver an impression of either lack of education and tech/business savvy or laziness. None of which is positive for instilling confidence or encouraging others to want to do business with you.

5) Responding Promptly

You should do your best to respond to your business e-mail as quickly as possible. This is a customer service issue that should not be underestimated. By not responding promptly you seem to be unorganized, uncaring or worse yet you may risk being outperformed by your competitors who understand the importance of appearing efficient and on the ball.

7.3 Some Golden Rules of International Business Etiquette

1) Sticking Up for One's Image

When participating in international communication, everyone should be aware that in the eyes of the foreigners, one is not only representing one's own corporation, but also one's own nation and race. It is very important to leave a good impression in that no one can redo his first impression or take it back. What you wear and how you behave will reveal your social status and self-confidence. So, it is important to be properly attired, keep neat and clean for every occasion and maintain an erect posture, cheery facial expression and relaxed movements. People will derive the impression from the nonverbal communication.

First impression is enhanced by good listening habits and eye contact. Symbolic gestures, such as a wave or smile, suggest friendliness. Speaking of others positively or standing up to greet a visitor will help make a favorable impression.

2) Being Neither Humble nor Arrogant

Being neither humble nor arrogant is a basic principle of the etiquette that concerns foreign affairs. You should not be a lickspittle(奉承者) or megalomania(狂妄自大者). It is inappropriate for you to show either inferiority or superiority. Being cordial (热情的) and independent are equally important. In international communication we should uphold justice and protect our cultural benefits and dignity under all circumstances.

3) Seeking Common Points while Reserving Difference

It will be much easier for people from different cultures to communicate and avoid misunderstanding if they observe intercultural convention and reach a consensus. Meanwhile, diversities in different cultures, e.g. special etiquette and customs, should be understood and respected. It will be beneficial for both sides if they understand the differences rather than judge them. Seeking common points while reserving difference is the most viable(切实可行的) way of communicating with foreigners.

4) When in Rome, Do as Romans Do

There is a proverb "When in Rome, do as Romans do". That's to say, "Don't set your own rules when you are someone's guest." The importance of local knowledge should never be underestimated. It can not only save you from embarrassment, but your foreign business partners are likely to appreciate your effort. When doing business travel in other nations, show courtesy to people wherever they are and observe their local social norms. In Japan, for instance, people may openly ask about private questions concerning your salary and the size of your home, which Americans consider very rude. The best bet is to observe the behavior of the locals and recognize that they may do many things differently.

"When in Rome, do as Romans do" is a good guideline. If travelling interculturally on business, one should always familiarize themselves beforehand with the local customs of the destination.

5) Being Punctual

Being punctual is a virtue every businessman should have. Being punctual is a good way to make a positive impression. It's commonly admitted that punctual people are considered dependable and showing up on time indicates your respect for others. Instead, being late for meetings or missing deadline just hurts your image. In the business world, "time is money" and companies may fine their employees for tardiness to business meetings.

Meanwhile, the cultural differences in the concept of time should be paid enough attention to. In some cultures, The scheduled time for a meeting allows for some flexibility, while in other cultures arriving late for a business appointment will jeopardize a business deal. For example, Germans are well-known for their punctuality. In many African and South American countries, however, scheduled appointments are often treated like a general guideline rather than something one has to strictly abide by.

Since some cultures are more time-conscious than others, it is always suggested to be punctual at first and simultaneously adopt a relaxed attitude towards time management. Even if you are always on time, your business partners may not take the appointed time for a business meeting as seriously as you do.

6) Respecting one's Privacy

In most eastern countries it is relatively usual to ask people personal questions to show concern, while Westerners, especially English speaking people, frown on being asked about personal matters. Our Chinese and some other Asian people prefer to show concern by asking questions about others' health, family, kids, and marriage, while people in western countries don't want to talk about these matters with others, especially strangers. They think these are their own business or privacy. Taboo topics such as age, money, religion and marriage are "forbidden zones" for Westerners; topics ranging from hobbies, sports and jobs to TV programs and holidays outing are quite safe for both Easterners and Westerners. In Britain, starting a conversation with the weather will always be appropriate. For example, he or she can say: "Lovely day, isn't it? Good weather, isn't it?"

In case you have to ask personal questions, you can begin by saying, "Excuse me for asking personal questions" or "Would you mind my asking some personal questions?"

7) Ladies First

It has its origins in Western European etiquette, basically the rules of conduct in society. In a number of situations, it was (and largely still is!) deemed correct behavior to give ladies precedence over gentlemen. This is for instance the case when serving food or drinks at a table: one serves the ladies firstly, then the other guests, then the host. However, the men have to be ahead of the ladies when they are expected to choose the table, to open the door of a car or render other services. When entering an unknown place, or when exiting a building, the man is to go first as well. The reasoning is that if any danger lurks on the other side of the door, the strong man can defend the poor defenseless damsel.

On the street, men almost always walk or cross the street on the side of the ladies which is closer to the traffic. But if a man walks with two ladies, he should walk in between them.

Although the custom is followed by fewer people than in the past, especially among the younger generation, women of all ages still appreciate this courtesy and it is regarded as one of the most important good manners in intercultural business.

8) Taking Good Care of the Environment

Taking good care of the environment is the basic social ethics that a person should have. With the increasing global awareness of the role of environmental factors playing in economic development, environmental protection has already received more attention and become one of the main concerns in the global stage nowadays.

In effect, each one of us has an obligation to protect the environment that all mankind rely on for existence. "China highly values ecological and envitonmental protection. Guided by the conviction that lucid water and lush mountains are invaluable assets, the country advocates harmonious coexistence between humans and nature, and stick to the path of green and sustainable development." (China Daily: 2018.07) We should pay special attention to the following seven aspects:

(1) Don't damage the natural environment;

(2) Don't maltreat animals;

(3) Don't damage public property;

(4) Don't litter;

(5) Don't spit everywhere;

(6) Don't smoke everywhere;

(7) Don't make loud noises in public places.

9) Taking Right Side as the Superior One

In a dinner party, the honored guest will be arranged to sit on the right of the host in China. In some countries like Thailand and Islamic countries, the left hand is considered unclean and should not be used to eat, receive gifts, or shake hands. Arabs traditionally use the right hand for all public functions—including shaking hands, eating, drinking, and passing objects to another person. In global business communication, it is safe to take the right side as the superior side.

Chapter 7 International Business Etiquette

In general, etiquette embodies one country's politics, practice and culture. It varies from culture to culture. In some countries people are more tolerant, while in other countries people stick to their traditional customs. The general rules of etiquette we discuss above will guide you to behave with courtesy and consideration in international communication. The most essential etiquette rule is: when in doubt, treat other people as you would want to be treated. As Confucius—the ancient Chinese saint relates, "don't do unto others what you don't want others do unto you."

Exercises

Ⅰ. **Questions for Discussion**

1. What is etiquette? Could you please list some examples in your life?
2. Is intercultural business etiquette important? Why?
3. Do you know something about Western table manners? How the forks and knives should be properly used?
4. When visiting a foreign family, what should be kept in mind to avoid cultural misunderstanding and embarrassment?
5. When visiting a foreigner's home, what should be taken into consideration when preparing a gift for a bussiness partner from another culture?

Ⅱ. **Comprehension Check**

Decide whether the following statements are true(T) or false(F)

_____ 1. What is considered good etiquette in one country must be considered extremely bad manners in another country.

_____ 2. Etiquette codes prescribe and restrict the ways in which people interact with each other, based on the respect for other people and the accepted customs of a society.

_____ 3. In North America and Europe, bowing is considered an appropriate and popular greeting form.

_____ 4. Even most Americans and British prefer a firm handshake than hugging and kissing.

_____ 5. It is OK to use a knife to convey food to the mouth.

_____ 6. We should attach greater importance to some guidelines for business etiquette than to some particular customs in some countries.

_____ 7. The dressing in business world is not very important because most people will not judge you from your appearance.

_____8. Hindus avoid beef and most of them are strict vegetarians.

_____9. The messages a gift sends definitely have something to do with the cost of it.

_____10. Large attachment should never be attached to your e-mail.

Ⅲ. **Vocabulary**

Complete the following sentences with the words given below and each word can be used only once.

| etiquette | fundamental | knowledgeable | guideline | privacy |
| conspicuous | hospitable | address | promptly | appropriate |

1. The people there are very _____ ; the guests from faraway will receive warm welcome when entering their homes.
2. _____ refers to guidelines which control the way a responsible individual should behave in the society.
3. He believes better relations with China are _____ to the well-being of the area.
4. We have had a very pleasant trip in Peking because the _____ guide told us a lot of historic stories.
5. _____ gift is essential for establishing the initial business relationship in some countries.
6. I gave her a few _____ on how to look after a kitten.
7. If someone or something is _____ , people can see or notice them very easily.
8. In business situations, it is suggested that you never _____ people using their given name for the first meeting in Japan.
9. By responding to business e-mail _____ shows you are organized and polite.
10. We build _____ into every product we make, so you can enjoy great experiences that keep your personal information safe and secure.

Ⅳ. **Translation**

Translate the Chinese phrases into English and vice versa.

1. 人不可貌相。
2. 良好的礼貌是由微小的牺牲组成。
3. 善有善报
4. 人类命运共同体
5. 入乡随俗
6. Don't do unto others what you don't want others do unto you.
7. The way you dress affects the way you are perceived and the way you are perceived

is the way you are treated.

8. Etiquette represents order, norms and values.
9. Be swift to hear, slow to speak.
10. One's courtesy is a mirror reflecting his portrait.

V. Case Analysis

Read the following cases and try to answer the questions afterwards.

Case 1

When President George Bush went to Japan with leading American businessmen, he made explicit and direct demands on Japanese leaders, which violated Japanese etiquette. To the Japanese, it was rude and a sign of ignorance or desperation to make direct demands. Some analysts believed it severely damaged the negotiations and confirmed to the Japanese that Americans are barbarians.

Questions for discussion:

What led to the misunderstanding between American and Japanese businessmen? How could they avoid the misunderstanding?

Case 2

A senior project manager for a U.S. tech company was concerned about whether his two-month implementation schedule should be modified to accommodate the holy month of Ramadan. Concerned with potential delay, his VP decided to proceed with "business as usual" and scheduled meetings and production nonetheless.

The U.S. project team faced not only absent team members, but questions about their disrespect for Islam. The implementation was subsequently delayed three months, then six months. Numerous U.S. deadlines were missed, penalties were assessed, and promotions lost.

Question for discussion:

How could this situation have been avoided?

VI. Role-Play Activities

Situation: One of your American friend is visiting China and you invite his/her family to dinner at your home. As a Chinese host/hostess, how will you treat them with our Chinese hospitality appropriately? As American friends, what are the proper etiquette when visiting Chinese family? You are required to act out the whole scenario including inviting by phone call, deciding on an appropriate gift, friends' greeting and dinning in Chinese family. (3-4 students are needed as a group for the role-play)

VII. Video Watching

Friends《六人行》

Chapter 8 Customs and Etiquette of Some Countries

As global business continues to expand and bring people closer, the most important element of successful business outcomes may be the appreciation and respect for regional, country, and cultural differences known as cultural diversity. Intercultural communication has become critical elements required for all international business executives, managers, and employees. To get to know the different customs and etiquette is an important way to broaden people's internationalization visions. In this Chapter, we will present the primary customs and etiquette in Oriental culture, Occidental culture, Middle-Eastern culture and Main African culture.

8.1 Oriental Culture

Diversity abounds in Oriental countries. With a multitude of races, languages and religions, Oriental offers a cornucopia of cultures. They have a lot in common in customs and etiquette as well as many differences. Generally, Orientals place a great deal of importance on relationship. The building of long lasting relationship is tantamount(相等的) for business success in Oriental countries. Also, "face" plays a great important role in building relationship. Here we take the main cultural features in Chinese, Japanese and Korean cultures as examples.

8.1.1 Chinese Culture

Chinese culture, long in history, varied in form and rich in content, has remained one of the most original, ingenious, and vital traditions among all civilizations. Chinese culture is gaining worldwide acceptance nowadays.

1) Chinese Concept of "Face"

The concept of "saving face" is inherent in this region. It is impossible to understand Chinese personal behavior without attempting to understand "face". "Face" is commonly viewed as a kind of conceit or vanity, a desire never to be seen as stupid or wrongheaded. Actually, it is a more complex concept than this. It is an unwritten set of rules by which people in society cooperate to avoid unduly damaging each other's prestige and self-respect.

For instance, in bargaining for a business deal, each side expects the other to take his or her "face" into account. Thus if a hard bargain is struck, and one party seems to have suffered a tactical defeat, the winning party should make some token concessions to save the others' "face". If no such arrangement is made, the loser may feel justly aggrieved(愤愤不平的,受委屈的) and try to avoid dealing with the other party in the future.

The importance of "face" in China helps to smooth out ruffled personal relations between Chinese and foreigners, because the Chinese will be pleased with a "face-saving" gesture, whereas it may mean little to the foreigners to make it. And Chinese will go to great lengths to save "face" and avoid embarrassment because face-losing is not easily forgotten nor is it easily forgiven.

2) Chinese Sages

Chinese culture has aroused wide interest throughout the whole world and many scholars endeavor to seek the quintessence of the teaching of ancient oriental sages such as *Lao Zi* and *Confucius*, *Mencius* in an attempt to discover the reasons for the success of Chinese culture. Confucianism represents the way of life followed by Chinese people for over 2,000 years. The influence of Confucianism is so predominant that if anyone should be asked to characterize in one word traditional Chinese life and culture, the word would be "Confucian". Primarily a code of ethics and a system of philosophy, Confucianism has left its mark on Chinese politics and government, family and society, art and literature. Daoism, along with Confucianism, is one of the two major indigenous religion-philosophical traditions that have shaped Chinese life for more than 2,000 years. Daoism is concerned with the ritual worship of the Way, which is the course, the principle, the substance, and the standard of all things, to which all must conform.

Many Chinese enterprises apply the tenets of ancient Chinese sages to the management of their companies, which proves impressively effective; and Western businesses are also alert to some of these trends.

3) Relationship (*Guanxi*)

As explained in Wikipedia, relationship (*Guanxi*, 关系) plays a fundamental role within the Confucian doctrine, which sees the individual as part of a community and a set of family, hierarchical and friendly relationship. In particular, there is a focus on tacit mutual commitments, reciprocity(相互性) and trust, which are the grounds of *Guanxi* and *Guanxi* networks. These "special relationship" or "connection" subtly define the Chinese moral code and play a central role in shaping and developing day-to-day business transactions by allowing inter-business relationship and relationship between businesses and the government to grow.

There is the view that the value and effectiveness of the *Guanxi* have greatly deteriorated, as the Chinese economy has become increasingly marketized, privatized and competitive. In industries that have been substantially deregulated or privatized, or where there is vigorous competition, business is business, and *Guanxi* has been neutralized or marginalized.

Doing business in China, on the surface, does not seem to be much different from doing business in the Western world. But in reality, the heavy reliance on relationship and collectivist way of thinking still prevails. Western companies have to make themselves known to the Chinese before any business can take place and this relationship does not simply concern companies but includes a relationship between individuals at a personal level and most importantly, the relationship is an ongoing process that needs to be maintained.

8.1.2 Japanese Culture

Japan is a hierarchical country. The Japanese are very conscious of age and status. Everyone has a distinct place in the hierarchy, be it the family unit, the extended family, a social or a business situation.

1) Greeting Etiquette

Greeting in Japan is very formal and ritualized. It is important to show the correct amount of respect and deference to someone based upon their status relative to your own. If at all possible, wait to be introduced. It can be seen as impolite to introduce yourself, even in a large gathering. While foreigners are expected to shake hands, the traditional form of greeting is the bow. How far you bow depends upon your relationship to the other person as well as the situation. The deeper you bow, the more respect you show. A foreign visitor may bow the head slightly, since no one expects foreigners to generally understand the subtle nuances of bowing.

2) Deferring to Elders

Japanese culture values its elders for the wisdom and experience they provide to the company. Age equals rank in Japan, so the older the person, the more important he is. The oldest person in a group is always revered and honored. In a social situation, they will be served first.

For example, it's customary in a meeting in Japan to always direct one's initial comments to the highest-ranking person present. One never disagrees with him and always gives him his due attention. In Japan, people greet each other by bowing, which is the most standard greeting manner. When you bow to others, you should always bow deepest to the most senior man.

3) Japanese Concept of "Face"

"Face" is also quite important in Japan. Especially, when you are having a meeting, the elder Japanese will pay more attention to their "face". Saving face is crucial in Japanese society. The Japanese believe that turning down someone's request causes embarrassment and face-losing to the other person.

If the request cannot be agreed to, they will say "It's inconvenient" or "It's under consideration". "Face" is a mark of personal dignity and means having high status with one's peers. The Japanese will never try to do anything to cause face-losing. Therefore, they do not openly criticize, insult, or put anyone on the spot. Face can be lost, taken away, or earned through praise and thanks.

8.1.3 Korean Culture

Korea has long been known as the "land of morning calm". Korea is a peninsula(半岛) surrounded by three seas: the Yellow Sea to the west, the Sea of Japan to the east, and the East China Sea to the south. To the north lie Manchuria and a small strip of Russian Siberia.

1) Social Ranking

South Korean culture is hierarchical and one's social status determines how one is treated. One of the first questions South Koreans ask each other when they meet for the first time is age. One common practice is to give up your seat on the bus for an older person who is standing. At dinner, the eldest person sits first and eats and drinks before anyone else can begin. Anyone older must always be addressed with honorifics, even among acquaintances. No one would think of calling an older person by their first name, much less a grandfather or grandmother. Bowing to them is really a traditional way of greeting.

2) Visiting & Dining Etiquette

It is customary to bring a small gift when visiting a South Korean home. It's better to bring a small token and not an ostentatious object that calls attention to you. Fruits, flowers, and chocolates are popular gifts for these occasions. South Koreans generally sit, eat, and sleep on the floor, so you will be expected to remove your shoes upon entering a South Korean home or restaurants. Bare feet may be offensive to people of the older generations, so it's best to wear socks when visiting and be sure they're clean and free of holes.

There is some etiquette we should know while eating with a Korean family. The eldest at the table eats first. No one even picks up his or her chopsticks until the eldest does. Guests sit on cushions around a low table. Many different foods are served, each cut into bite-sized pieces. Each person has his own bowl of rice, but helps himself to other foods directly from the serving dishes.

In addition to chopsticks, South Koreans regularly use soup-spoons at meals. The chopsticks are used primarily for side dishes, while the spoon is used for soup and rice. Unlike in Japan, it's not appropriate to pick up your rice bowl while eating. All plates and bowls should stay on the table. During the meal, rest your chopsticks and spoon on top of a dish. When you have finished eating, lay the chopsticks or spoon on the table to indicate that you have completed the meal. Never stick chopsticks or spoons in a bowl of rice. This is done only during ancestral memorial services.

Rather than pouring their own drinks, Koreans pour for one another. It is a bad breach of etiquette to pour your own drink. Use both hands when pouring a drink for someone, because it shows respect. Though filling a companion's glass with beer or *soju* (similar to vodka) is appropriate, it's essential that the glass is completely empty before pouring. This may seem like a trivial concern, but will count for a lot in the eyes of your South Korean friends.

Among young people, the person who issues the invitation usually pays. If you're out with a group, the bill is split and everyone pitches in.

3) Patriarchal Control

Korean society is highly patriarchal(家长的) since the Confucian system was introduced from China. Fathers are responsible for their families and must be both obeyed and revered by everyone. Even ancestral fathers are honored. The custom is called filial piety and even today elements of it remain among Koreans. For instance, at dinner the eldest person sits first and eats and drinks before anyone else can begin. Anyone older must always be addressed with honorifics(敬语), even among acquaintances. Bowing to them is the really traditional way of greeting. Hard work, obedience to family, protection of the family, and proper decorum among family members are highly valued in Korea, even in the modern world.

8.2 Occidental Culture

Occidental culture, sometimes equated with Western civilization and European civilization, is characterized by a host of artistic, philosophic, literary and legal themes and traditions. It is a term used very broadly to refer to a heritage of social norms, ethical values, traditional customs, belief systems, political systems and specific artifacts and technologies that have some origin or association with Europe. It also applies beyond Europe to countries and cultures whose histories are strongly connected to Europe by immigration, colonization, or influence.

Occidental culture includes countries in the Americas and Australia, whose language and demographic ethnicity majorities are Europeans. The development of Occidental culture has been strongly influenced by Christianity.

8.2.1 American Culture

American culture is unique because it is nurtured, formed and developed under certain conditions, which are characteristically American. The major factors contributing to the making of this new nation and the forming of a new culture are the hard environment, ethnic diversity and plural religion, which is quite different from other nations in the world. What is

Chapter 8 Customs and Etiquette of Some Countries

more, these elements are still influencing the American culture.

1) Ethnic Diversity

The population of the United States is over 300 million people of mixed races and heritage. Although the population is predominantly of European descent, the country has been a welcoming beacon to immigrants from virtually every country and culture in the world. English is the predominant language, although languages from many foreign countries are spoken within cultural enclaves throughout the United States, with the majority of Americans are Christians.

As a land of immigrants, the United States has benefited from diverse cultures in many ways. America has grown beyond the early "melting pot" idea that viewed different ethnic groups as blending into one big culture. This meant that some groups lost their valued heritage to become part of a homogeneous culture mixture.

2) Plural Religion

The fundamental American belief in individual freedom and the right of individuals to practice their own religion is at the center of religious experience in the United States. The great diversity of ethnic backgrounds has produced religious pluralism; almost all of the religions of the world are now practiced in the United States. Christianity is the dominant religion in Americans and Protestant is predominating. All individuals are equal before God and they believe they can communicate directly to God so they can share the same idea. Under the Protestant, many new ones are formed and different explanations produce different sects of religion. Churches are independent and American religion is no longer religion secular. The institution permits the practice of religion and the political power is separate from religion. So there are more religions in the United States than in other countries.

3) Greeting

When meeting someone for the first time, it is customary to shake hands, both for men and for women. Good friends may briefly embrace, although the larger the city is, usually the more formal the behavior is. Kissing is not common, and men never kiss other men.

When communicating with an American, offer a firm handshake, lasting 3 to 5 seconds, upon greeting and leaving. Maintain good eye contact during your handshake. If you are meeting several people at once, maintain eye contact with the person you are shaking hands with, until you are moving on to the next person. Good eye contact during business and social conversation shows interest, sincerity and confidence. Business cards are generally exchanged during introduction. A smile is a sign of friendliness, and in rural areas you may be greeted with a "hello" rather than a handshake.

Americans will usually introduce themselves by their first name and last name (such as "Hello, I'm John Smith"), or, if the setting is very casual, by their first name only ("Hi, I'm John"). The common response when someone is introduced to you is "Pleased to meet you". Americans normally address everyone they meet in a social or business setting by their first name. However, you should always address your college professors by their titles and last names (such as Professor Jones), unless they ask you to do otherwise.

4) Alcohol License

Many restaurants in the Unite States (except for fast food restaurants) have a license to serve alcohol. Beer and wine are always available, and at some restaurants hard liquor (such as vodka or whisky) is also available. Restaurants that serve hard liquor are said to have "a full bar". The legal age for drinking alcohol in the Unite States is 21. If you look young, be prepared to show proof of your age when ordering alcohol.

5) Tip-Giving

There are only a few situations where tipping is expected. The most common one is at restaurants. American restaurants do not add a service charge to the bill. Therefore it is expected that the customer will leave a tip for the server. The common practice is to leave a tip that is equal to 15% of the total bill for acceptable service, and about 20% for superior service. If the service is unusually poor, then you could leave a smaller tip, about 10%.

There are other professions where tipping is expected, such as hair dressers, taxi drivers, hotel porters, parking valets, and bartenders. The general rule is to tip approximately 15% of the bill. In situations where there is no bill (as with hotel porters and parking valets), the tip may range from $1 to $5, depending on the type of establishment and on how good the service is.

6) Smoking Restrictions

Smoking is prohibited in many places. It is not allowed in any public buildings, on any public transportation (including airplane flights within the United States), in shops, movie theaters, schools, and office buildings. The general rule is if you are indoors, then you probably are not allowed to smoke. The exceptions are bars, nightclubs, and some restaurants. If a restaurant does allow smoking, it will only be in an area that is designated for smokers. If you are with someone, even outdoors, it is polite to ask permission to smoke before lighting a cigarette or cigar.

8.2.2 British Culture

British culture is influenced by its history as a developed state, a liberal democracy and a great power. But this is just a stereotype which never applies to the majority of the British people, and really has little validity today. The things that people know about the UK (which they will probably call simply Britain or, wrongly, England) may have little to do with how most real British people live their lives today.

The UK is one nation, with a single passport, and a single government having sovereignty over it all, but as the fullname of the nation suggests, it is made up of different elements. It includes 4 parts within the one nation-state: the island of Great Britain which is made up of England, Scotland and Wales, and Northern Ireland, a province on the neighboring island of Ireland, each of which has its distinct customs, cultures and symbolism.

1) Royal Traditions

Although the British royal family has no real power, they are still very important to British people. In many ways they represent everything that is traditionally British.

British have three royal traditions. Playing the flute is one of the royal traditions. Every morning after breakfast, the Queen listens to the playing of a flute by the royal flutist who does so outside the dining-hall for a quarter of an hour. This is a tradition inherited from Queen Victoria.

The change of the Queen's guard is another of the royal traditions. There are two places in which the ceremonies take place. One ceremony is in front of Buckingham Palace. The other is at Whitehall. Both take place at 11 a.m.

The third royal tradition involves only the monarch. Annually, the British Queen makes a parliamentary speech, the ceremony for which is rather solemn.

2) UK's Weather

The weather is one of the things Britain is most famous for. British weather is very changeable, and you can get all the seasons in one day in Britain. It can be a very nice bright sunny morning, T-shirt weather, and then by lunchtime it can be dark, grey, a little bit chilly, and you need an overcoat or a raincoat.

3) British Stereotypes

There are lots of stereotypes and misconceptions related to the British. Some are true, but some are completely made up.

For example, all British people like to queue. Ther are thousands of queues that you can't avoid in most cities. A bank or a bus stop both require a level of courtesy, that is to say members of the public in Britain are brought up in a culture that has a tendency to queue in a range of everyday situations. Since this is the norm, those who break it or "queue jumpers" are often frowned upon.

Furthermore, all British people hate other nationalities. British people like to think they were once rulers of the world, so some of this quest for global notoriety still lingers up until the present day. However, nowadays most of the comments made about other nations are meant in jest(笑话). In fact, the average British are very fond of friendly rivalry with other nationalities.

Moreover, all British people speak the Queen's English. The English language is often misconstrued as being only understood as an elite expression of lords and ladies. In the days of Kings and Queens, the language was certainly more Dickensian, but modern Britain is an eclectic(折中的) blend of different sounds. In fact, the true vernacular is refreshingly diverse in its slang, and you'll probably surprise the person on the street with how good your English is.

8.2.3 French Culture

France, the largest nation in Western Europe, has an area of about 211,000 square miles (546,490 square kilometers). It has been said that "everyone has two homes—his own and France". For centuries, France has been a wellspring of inspiration in art, music, and literature. For centuries, France has been a fountainhead for many of the world's great ideas. The language of the country is still a second language for many cultivated people everywhere.

1) French Love

French is known as the "language of romance". People associate French with love. Paris is the capital of love and the most romantic city in the world, with its beautiful architecture, cleanness, history, drama and rivers. It just dazzles us with its whole atmosphere, which is not easy to describe in words to someone who hasn't been there yet. Fashion is very important in France, as style is more important than looks. In France, it's not about how much you have, but who you are and what your thoughts are, which is why it's also such an artistic place. The city is filled with details that make it unique. For instance, big supermarkets are banned, so people buy baguettes at small grocery stores and take them to their work while riding a bicycle. This may seem like a picturesque image to you, but it's what you get to see every day in Paris.

Enjoying life is crucial in France, which is the reason why after work, a lot of people enjoy just sitting in the park and having a picnic.

2) Diverse Cuisine

French cuisine is extremely diverse, considered to be one of the world's most refined cuisines. French techniques are generally used as the basis for all European cooking and the yardstick by which food is measured throughout the Western world. With recipes ranging from creamy sauces and rich pastries to hearty stews and warming soups, French cooking has inspired and influenced the techniques of chefs through the ages.

The variety in French cuisine is supported by the French passion for good food in all its forms, France's extraordinary range of different geographies and climates which support the local production of all types of ingredients, and France's long and varied history. In many ways, an understanding of the culture of French food is an understanding of France itself.

3) Taboo Topics

Frenchmen are talkative. There is rarely a moment of silence, except when the topic under discussion has been exhausted, and nothing new has been introduced. You'll find that conversations often shift into spirited debates.

Frenchmen like to talk about these topics: food, art, music, sports, philosophy and current events. But they will try to avoid some topics. The taboo topics are religion, politics and sex. It is extremely a bad manner to ask an individual about his political leanings or how he vote.

The French also enjoy a verbal conflict. They are very interested in different opinions and can provoke you to express what you really feel. They like people who are sincere and who don't talk about superficial stuff. Therefore, if you have a different opinion from them, they may question you and try to get you to talk so that they can try to see your point of view.

There are three main conversation rules: do not hurt the person's feelings; do not shock them unnecessarily; do not attack them. Silence is not good. If there is too long a pause, the hostess will launch another conversation topic. It is very common for many people to express their opinions at the same time.

8.2.4 German Culture

Germany lies in the center, the heart, of Europe. It is a heartland that has varied greatly in size during the years of its existence as a nation. Germany can be divided into three main landform regions, the northern lowlands, the central highlands, and the southern alpine, or mountain region.

1) The Image

Most Germans people speak in a very direct manner, in that foreigners always tend to think Germans are rude, and arrogant. Actually, a German will almost always let you know what he/she really thinks. However, you should keep your manners conservative until you "learn the ropes".

It is also a widespread stereotype that Germans do not have a sense of humor. To a certain extent this can be true and some Germans even take humor seriously and some do not appreciate sarcasm. Jokes tend to be made about the system rather than being aimed at individuals.

2) German Rules

The Germans came relatively late to democracy and have long lived under a system which controlled their lives to a high degree. Most tend to play by the rules and thus appear to outsiders as very conservative.

In Germany, there are rules to almost anything: there are certain times when your dog is allowed to bark, certain times when you can cut your grass, certain places where you are allowed to wash your car (Don't dare to do it in front of your own garage. It is forbidden by law.) and much more... However, it also applies to German culture: no rules without exceptions, but there are few. If you really want to break the "rules", make sure that your neighbor is not watching.

Moreover, it is true that Germans consider punctuality a virtue. Germans are extremely punctual, particularly business professionals, and arriving late may put you in a compromising position. An appointment at 10 a.m. means exactly at 10 a.m., not earlier or later. Therefore, if you realize that you are not going to arrive somewhere at the appointed time, call and announce that you will be late.

However, as to any other rule, there is an exception: among friends, it is considered

Chapter 8 Customs and Etiquette of Some Countries

OK if you show up 15 minutes late sometimes, if this does not become a habit. If you are invited to someone's house, whether you are invited for coffee or a meal, it is customary to bring along a small gift for the host or hostess. Popular examples are a bottle of wine, some chocolates or flowers.

3) German Meals

While many Americans eat only two meals a day, skipping breakfast or lunch, the Germans have only in modern times switched to three meals a day down from five. Coffee and pastries make up a second breakfast, while late-afternoon sausage and cheese dishes fill in until the evening smorgasbord-like meal.

Open-faced sandwiches are served frequently and are meant to be eaten with a knife and fork. Lunch is the biggest meal of the day, and these sandwiches make nice, lighter dinner fare.

4) Family and Marriage

As in many other Western countries, family life has undergone many changes. In contrast to past generations, when families had numerous children, some one-fifth of married German couples never become parents, and most of the remainders have only one or two children. Thus, German birth rate is low and below the replacement level. More people are also living together before or instead of marrying. The number of marriage is declining, and the number of divorce have increased. About one-fourth of all births now occur outside of marriage. Changing marriage patterns have also influenced gender roles. Traditionally, German families had highly differentiated gender roles within marriage—men worked outside the home and women undertook most homemaking activities and childcare. During the last decades of the 20th century, however, this pattern shifted, with more than two-thirds of working-age women employed outside the home—though they still are underrepresented within the elite professions.

8.3 Middle-Eastern Culture

The Middle East is a transcontinental region centered on Western Asia, Turkey (both Asian and European) and Egypt (which is mostly in North Africa). Saudi Arabia is geographically the largest Middle Eastern nation while Bahrain is the smallest. Religion plays a very important role in all the countries of the Middle East. The predominant religion for the Arab and Middle Eastern countries is Islam.

8.3.1 Egyptian Culture

The Arab Republic of Egypt is a new name for the very ancient land of Egypt. Over 5,000 years have passed since the first Pharaoh ruled, but the same kind of oxen pictured on the walls of early tombs can still be seen drawing plows in Egyptian fields. Egypt is the second most populous country of Africa. Peasant farmers called fellahin (singular: fellah) make up over 60 percent of the population. But less than 4 percent of Egypt's land is suitable for farming.

1) Dressing

The fellah wears a lose, long cotton robe, which is called *gallabiyea*, loose cotton pants, and a wool cap, which he makes himself. For special events he makes a turban by folding a white sash around the cap. Flat, yellow slippers complete the fellah's outfit.

The wife of the fellah wears dresses with long sleeves and trailing flounces and a black veil, which she sometimes uses to cover her face. On market days and other special occasions the women wear earrings, necklaces, bracelets and ankles. These ornaments are usually made of beads, silver, glass, copper, or gold. They make a pleasant musical sound as the women walk along the dusty lanes of the village.

2) Religions

Over 90 percent of Egyptians are Muslims. The skylines of Egypt's cities are filled with minarets, the towers of mosques. Five times a day the voice of the muezzin (prayer-caller) calls the faithful to prayer. When Muslims pray they face Mecca(麦加,在沙特阿拉伯,为伊斯兰教圣地), the city in Saudi Arabia where Mohammed was born. The Muslims pray to Allah (God) declaring in his prays that "there is no God but the one god and Mohammed is His Prophet". During the holy month of Ramadan, one of the 12 months of the Islamic lunar calendar, Muslims fast from sunrise to sunset. Muslims are also obliged to give alms(救济金) to the poor. At least once in a lifetime, when it is financially and physically possible, a Muslim is called upon to make a pilgrimage(朝圣之旅) to Mecca.

About 8 percent of the Egyptians are Christians. Also there are small groups of Roman Catholics, Greek Orthodox, Armenians and Protestants in Egypt.

3) Greeting

There is some special etiquette in Egypt. Greeting is based on both class and the religion of the person. It is best to follow the lead of the Egyptian you are meeting. Handshakes are the customary greeting among individuals of the same sex. Handshakes are somewhat limp and prolonged, although they are always given with a hearty smile and direct eye contact. Once a relationship has developed, it is common to kiss on one cheek between the people of the same sex. In any greeting between men and women, the woman must extend her hand first. If she does not, a man should bow his head in greeting.

4) Visiting

If you are invited to an Egyptian's home for dinner, dress well and conservatively. Appearances are important to Egyptians. You would normally remove your shoes before entering. Bring good quality chocolates, sweets or pastries to the hostess. Do not give flowers, which are usually reserved for weddings or the ill unless you know that the hosts would appreciate them. A small gift for the children shows affection. Always give gifts with the right hand or both hands if the gift is heavy. Gifts are not opened when received.

Before the dinner, wait for the host or hostess to tell you where to sit. Eat with the right hand only. It is considered a sincere compliment to take second helpings. Always show appreciation for the meal. Salting your food is considered an insult. Leave a small amount of food on your plate when you have finished eating, otherwise they will keep filling it up for you!

5) Marriage

Marriage has special importance to Egyptians. The ancient Egyptians were the first people who stated marriage laws in the world. They regarded marriage as a civil and legal relationship. The ancient Egyptian laws gave the right of divorce to women as well as men. The wife was respected greatly, and she had high prestige.

Egyptians consider marriage as the most important event in their lives. They assume marriage is the main method to protect youth from any sacred relationship. Moreover, marriage is a religious imposition and it reinforces society's relationship. There is no doubt that marriage customs indicate the society's culture, behavioral patterns, thoughts and feelings.

8.3.2 Saudi Arabia Culture

Saudi Arabia is a vast country in area. It is almost four times the size of France and although much of the land is desert. There are also coastal plains, high mountains, and large cities. It is a rich country, whose wealth derives from the great reserves of oil lying beneath the surface. Historically, it is unique in having been the birthplace of Mohammed, the prophet of Islam, a faith that spreads beyond Saudi Arabia to much of Asia and Africa.

The vast majority of Saudi Arabia's people are Arabs. Almost all are Muslims of the Sunni branch of Islam and belong to the strictly orthodox *Wahhabi* sect. Islam is the state religion and plays an important role in the everyday life of the people. Arabic is the official language of the country. The people of Saudi Arabia may be divided according to their ways of life into two main groups: those who live in settled communities and those who are nomads or semi-nomads.

1) Characteristics

Regardless of their racial origins, the people have two common characteristics: they speak Arabic and are of the Moslem faith. They are intensely proud people and regard their independence both as individuals and as a nation as an absolute right. They have a deep respect for personal dignity and country, while their customs of generous hospitality are well known.

The precepts of Islam, together with deep-rooted traditions founded on the customs of centuries, give to the Arab a deep respect for social dignity and courtesy. It is a matter of habit rather than ostentation and it is, therefore, important for foreigners to familiarize themselves with local customs.

2) Greeting

In particular, every personal contact, in all spheres of life (casual or not, including telephone calls, entering shops and so on) begins with some form of courteous greeting. It is always much appreciated if foreigners take the trouble to learn the Arabic forms of greeting and response, which are, for this purpose, fairly standardized.

Saudi custom regarding greeting is rather ritualized. When entering a meeting full of people, a Saudi will greet each person individually with a handshake while standing. The same is expected of visitors. Furthermore, a person must always stand up to greet and shake the hand of the visitor of any kind. Omission of this phase of the social or business contact gives rise to automatic mild social offence so the dialogue "starts off on the wrong foot". It is customary in Saudi Arabia for male relatives and close family friends to greet one another by kissing and for them to hold hands while walking and talking together. On very rare occasions, these courtesies may be extended to male foreign visitors.

In Arabic, an individual is addressed by his or her first name, and any title he possesses. A "Dr. Ahmed Bin Al-Rahman" would be addressed as "Dr. Ahmed". The word "Bin" or "Ibn" means "son of" and may be present a number of times in a person's name, as Saudi names are indicators of genealogy(血统).

3) Conversation Etiquette

Light social conversation generally centers around health (the weather is unremarkable conversationally). It is generally safer at first to avoid asking about wife and family. However, most Arabs are considerate and could understand if a foreigner unwittingly makes a social blunder(错误).

When engaged in conversation, Saudis tend to stand much closer to one another than Americans, North Europeans, and East Asians do. Their conversational distance is more similar to that of Latin Americans and Southern Europeans. Arabs will also employ some body contact to emphasize a point or confirm that they have your attention. It is important not to draw back, however. This may be interpreted as a rebuff or rejection of what is being said. Respect is a value that is held very highly by the Arab people, and this shows in both business and social settings.

Talking with one's hands, or gesticulating wildly, may be considered impolite. It is also impolite to point the sole of the foot at the person to whom you are speaking. When tea and coffee are served, it could be considered impolite not to take at least one cup. When one has finished drinking, one should oscillate(摆动) the cup to signal that a refill is not desired. If one is doing business in the Kingdom during Ramadan, it is best to refrain from drinking and eating when in the company of someone observing the fast.

4) Women's Status and Dressing

The position of women in Saudi Arabia is far different from that of Western countries. From a fairly early age, they live in extreme privacy and are not normally seen by men other than their husbands and close male relatives. In the houses of the rich and poor alike, the women have separate quarters into which only intimate members of the family are permitted. Accordingly, mixed social gatherings or parties are rare. Women are expected to dress conservatively, with long skirts most appropriate, sleeves at elbow length or longer, and necklines that are unrevealing. It is generally uncommon for a Muslim man to shake hands with a woman or engage in the conversational body contact that is common when speaking to another man, although Saudis who have experiences with Western culture may be inclined to do so.

The custom of parade prevails in Saudi Arabia and women appear in public completely veiled from head to foot. It is most impolite to stare at them and on no account should they be photographed.

5) Hospitality

The Arabs are justifiably famous for their hospitality and, while the standards are set by custom, the Arab applies them with warmth that reflects his enjoyment in entertaining his guest. The most usual gesture for the entertainment of an individual or small group is the serving of coffee (usually unsweetened and heavily flavored with cardamom seed for the foreigner, a taste to be acquired). It is also common to serve tea (sweetened and without milk) or soft drinks in offices and shops when the occasion arises. It is impolite to refuse these important tokens of hospitality.

8.3.3 Iranian Culture

Iran, better known in the West until recently as Persia, is situated at one of the main crossroads linking Europe and the Middle East with Central Asia. The name Iran means "land of the Aryans"—a reference to the country's original settlers.

Nearly all Iranians are Muslims. There are some 20,000 Muslim mosques in the country, many of which are the ancient buildings of rare beauty. Small numbers of Christians, Jews, and Zoroastrians also practice their faiths.

Traditionally, most Iranians used to live in rural areas. Because of new opportunities in industry, many people moved from the countryside to the cities in search of a better way of life. Today about half of all Iran's people live in cities.

Iran is an ancient and proud civilization with its own customs and traditions. It is also a state where public behavior is strictly governed by laws. And it is an economy where personal relationship is the foundation of business dealings. It is important to bear these facts in mind when doing business there.

1) Business Etiquette

Iranians are polite and formal. If offered tea, you are expected to drink it or at least sip it. Don't ask for coffee unless you are offered. During the meeting, fruits or cakes are usually served, but you can take one only after your host has offered. Most meetings will begin with an ice-breaking personal conversation. In many instances it is considered rude to get down to business right away unless an issue is pressing. While your dealings may sometimes seem slow by Western standards both in a given meeting and over the course of the development of the deal you are negotiating you are laying the groundwork of personal trust which is very important in Iranian business dealings. Punctuality is considered a sign of respect, and meetings should start on time.

Men should wear conservative business attire, particularly in initial meetings. Iranian men particularly government workers do not wear ties, as the late Imam Khomeini declared them to be symbols of Western imperialism. After a period of time, more casual attire is acceptable. However, it is not recommended to dress more casually than your interlocutor. Shorts are never worn in public, even one is jogging. Short-sleeved shirts are acceptable in the summer as long as Ramadan or the mourning month of Moharram doesn't fall during the summer. If you cross you legs while sitting, be careful not to show the soles of your shoes.

2) Women's Status and Dressing

Women in public must be modestly dressed. Even though standard tends to be less strict for Western visitors than for locals, modest dress is still required by law and by social custom. Women should cover their hair and neck with a scarf and wear a loose-fitting coat that extends below the knee. Shoes should be closed and legs should be covered by pants or stockings.

On the other hand, women can do much of what men do in Iran—going out alone, driving cars, and working outside the home. Women can do business with men; however, women and men should not shake hands or have physical contact in public.

3) Gifting Etiquette

The exchange of gifts is not uncommon in business dealings which, after all, have a very significant personal element to them in Iran. Usually, pens, pins, books or small souvenirs of either your company or your country are appreciated. The most senior person should always receive the nicest gift.

8.4 Main African Cultures

The vast continent of Africa is so rich and diverse in its culture. Cultures change from one country to another, even within an individual country many different cultures can be found. Much of Africa's cultural activity centers on the family and the ethnic group. Art, music, and oral literature serve to reinforce existing religious and social patterns.

Africa was the birthplace of the human species between 8 million and 5 million years ago. Today, the vast majority of its inhabitants are of indigenous origin. People across the continent are remarkably diverse by just about any measure: they speak a vast number of different languages, practice hundreds of distinct religions, live in a variety of types of dwellings, and engage in a wide range of economic activities.

Europeans first settled in Africa in the mid-17th century near the Cape of Good Hope, at the southern end of the continent. More Europeans immigrated during the subsequent colonial period, particularly to present-day South Africa, Zimbabwe, and Algeria. South Asians also arrived during the colonial time. Their descendants, often referred to as Indians, are found largely in Uganda, Kenya, Tanzania, and South Africa.

8.4.1 South African Culture

The Republic of South Africa is one of the richest countries in the world. In 1867 an African boy playing on the banks of the Orange River discovered a beautiful pebble, later identified as a diamond. This discovery of diamonds changed the history of South Africa. Thousands of people poured into the territory to settle and strike it rich. In 1884 gold was discovered in the city of Johannesburg. The profits from the mines of diamond and gold were used to develop industries. Thus, the country became rich quickly.

The country has a diverse population: over 68 percent of the inhabitants are Africans; about 19 percent are whites, or Europeans; 10 percent are colored (mixed African and other races); and about 3 percent are Asians.

1) Greeting

There are several greeting styles in South Africa depending upon the ethnic heritage of the person you are meeting. When dealing with foreigners, most South Africans shake hands while maintaining eye contact and smiling. Some women do not shake hands and merely nod their heads, so it is best to wait for a woman to extend her hand. Men may kiss a woman they know well on the cheek in place of a handshake.

2) Gifting Etiquette

In general, South Africans give gifts for birthdays and Christmas. The 21st and the 40th

birthdays are often celebrated with a large party in which a lavish gift is given. It is common for several friends to contribute to this gift to help defray the cost. If you are invited to a South African's home, bring flowers, good quality chocolates, or a bottle of good South African wine to the hostess. Wrapping a gift nicely shows extra effort. Gifts are opened when received.

3) Visiting

If you are invited to a South African's house, you should arrive on time. If invited to a dinner, contact the hostess ahead of time to see if she would like you to bring a dish. You may wear casual clothes. This may include jeans or pressed shorts. It is a good idea to check with the host in advance. It is considered polite to offer to help the hostess with the preparation or clearing up after a meal is served.

4) Business Etiquette

South African business people tend to dress conservatively. Loud sports jackets and slacks are rarely seen at work. South African businesswomen tend to wear woolen or woven cotton blend suits in the cooler months of April through August. In the warmer months cotton or linen suits are appropriate. Men tend to favor medium or heavy woolen suits for year-round wear. South Africans are transactional and do not need to establish long-standing personal relationship before conducting business. If your company is not known in South Africa, a more formal introduction may help you gain access to decision-makers and not be shunted off to gatekeepers. Networking and relationship building are crucial for long-term business success. Most businessmen are looking for long-term business relationship. Although the country leans towards egalitarianism(平均主义), business people respect senior executives and those who have attained their position through hard work and perseverance. For the most part, South Africans want to maintain harmonious working relationship, so they avoid confrontations.

8.4.2　Kenya Culture

The vibrant Kenya Culture is a blend of diverse ethnic subcultures. It's influenced by ancient African customs and traditions, with modern beliefs and values making it uniquely Kenyan.

Some Kenyan ethnic communities have held on to their early African cultural practices while others have since drifted to modern practices. These have provided colorful traditions and a rich cultural heritage. This is expressed in the people's way of life as pertaining to their food, art, music, and cultural interaction with one another from the ones who value ancient traditions to the ones who value modern beliefs.

There's a big divide in some instances from one tribe to the other. The Maasai, Samburu, and Turkana are widely known for holding on to their traditional cultures. This is unlike the Kikuyu and other Kenyan tribes who have mainly embraced modern cultural values.

The Kenya government assures the protection and promotion of culture and cultural diversity among Kenyans. It has come up with a National Policy on Culture and Heritage. Cultural relativism plays an important role in bringing communities together and unifying the nation.

The diversity of Kenya culture can often be identified by different traditional and modern ways of life. These are evident in the Kenya people's food, fashion, artifacts, cultural festivals and the way they interact. Most of the urbanites have long adopted modern lifestyles or Western culture.

Exercises

I. **Questions for Discussion**

1. Please discuss what the concept of "face" means to Chinese people.
2. Try to illustrate how Confucianism has left its mark on Chinese politics and government, family and society, and art and literature.
3. Have you ever experienced any cultural conflicts when you are abroad? And how did you handle them?
4. Which cultural representation would you relate to the American Dream? Why?
5. Do you know any customs about the religions in Middle Eastern countries?

II. **Comprehension Check**

Decide whether the following statements are true (T) or false (F).

_____ 1. Many China enterprises apply the tenets of ancient Chinese sages to the management of their companies.

_____ 2. In Japan, to make a self-introduction in a large gathering can be seen as very polite.

_____ 3. Japanese people greet each other by shaking hands.

_____ 4. Bare feet are offensive to people of the older generations in Korean culture.

_____ 5. To American people, time is money.

Chapter 8 Customs and Etiquette of Some Countries

_____6. It is expected that the customers should leave a tip for the server in the American restaurants.

_____7. The British royal family has real power, so they are very important to the British people.

_____8. British weather is very changeable, and you can get all the seasons in one day in Britain.

_____9. French is known as the "language of romance".

_____10. The predominant religion for the Arab and Middle Eastern countries is Hinduism.

Ⅲ. **Vocabulary**

Choose the appropriate word from the word box to complete the sentence below and each word can be used only once.

| "face" | etiquette | transcontinental | tradition | peninsula |
| relationships | taboo | tenets | "melting pot" | conservatively |

1. Generally, Orientals place a great deal of importance on _____.
2. It is impossible to understand Chinese personal behavior without attempting to understand _____.
3. Many China enterprises apply the _____ of ancient Chinese sages to the management of their companies.
4. Greeting _____ in Japan is very formal and ritualized.
5. Korea is a _____ surrounded by three seas: the Yellow Sea to the west, the Sea of Japan to the east, and the East China Sea to the south.
6. America has grown beyond the early _____ idea that viewed different ethnic groups as blending into one big culture.
7. The changing of the Queen's guard is another British royal _____.
8. Religion, politics and sex are _____ topics in French.
9. The Middle East is a _____ region centered on Western Asia.
10. South African business people tend to dress _____. Loud sports jackets and slacks are rarely seen at work.

Ⅳ. **Translation**

Translate the following Chinese phrases into English and vice versa.

1. Confucianism

2. Daoism

3. greeting etiquette

4. melting pot

5. diverse cuisine

6. 禁忌话题

7. 穆斯林

8. 陈规旧俗

9. 职业装

10. 好望角

Ⅴ. Case Analysis

Case 1

A Japanese manager in an American company was told to give critical feedback to a subordinate during a performance evaluation. Because the Japanese are used to high context language and are uncomfortable with giving direct feedback, it took the manager five tries before he was direct enough for the American subordinate to understand.

Question:

What advice can you offer to the Japanese manager?

Case 2

In the following interaction, Jim is a student at a local university. He was born and raised in the united States. Akira is an exchange student from Japan. Jim and Akira are eating dinner together in a local restaurant. They have known each other for only a short time. Not only is Jim's style of communication overtly personal; he's also quite direct.

Jim: Hey buddy, what do you think of this American restaurant? I really like it.

Akira: Yes, Mr Jim. This is very nice.

Jim: I always prefer restaurants like this, kinda casual but good food. I come here a lot. Do you go out to eat much in Japan?

Akira: Japanese restaurants are nice, too.

Jim: Yeah, but do you go out to eat much?

Akira: Sure, Japanese people like restaurants.

Jim: Whenever I come here I usually order the same thing. It's kinda funny, but since I like it. I figure I may as well eat it. I have a lot of friends that do that.

Akira: Sure.

Chapter 8 Customs and Etiquette of Some Countries

Jim: Yeah, I was thinking the other day that since the dorm food sucks so bad, I should go out to eat more often.

Akira: Yes, that's a good idea.

——*Intercultural Communication* by Todd R. Armstrong

Questions:

Is there anything wrong with the conversation? Could you please analyse their different communication etiquette?

Ⅵ. Oral Presentation

Get the students to make a PowerPoint presentation about the various etiquette and customs in different countries on the basis of the following topics.

Greeting ways

Dining habits

Social ranking

Religion

Ⅶ. Video Watching

The Joy Luck Club《喜福会》

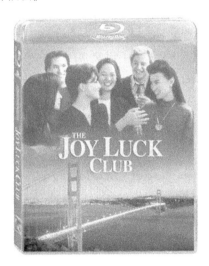

Supplementary Reading

Social Customs and Etiquette of Some OBOR Countries

1 Thailand

Thailand is located in the center of Southeast Asia and shares its borders with Cambodia, Laos, Malaysia, and Myanmar (formerly Burma). Thailand is an ethnic melting pot of peoples from surrounding lands. Chinese, Khmer, Laotian, Malaysian, and Vietnamese people have come together in this nation, intermarried, and merged into the Thai culture. This is especially true in urban areas like Bangkok, where Thai, Chinese, Malay, and even English are all spoken in the streets. Most Thai people are Buddhists, but there are also a fair number of Muslims and Christians. In the northern regions, "mountain peoples" continue to live with a fairly traditional lifestyle.

Thais are among the world's most tolerant people and will forgive your cultural faux pas as long as they are unintentional; however, there are two things that you must respect during your stay in Thailand: the royal family and religion.

While it is possible to discuss political problems, but one should never criticize the monarchy, and always stand while the National Anthem is played. Religious objects and sites, such as Buddha images and the wat (Buddhist temples) are sacred to the Thais. It is important for visitors to show respect by dressing conservatively whenever they visit a wat. Remove shoes and keep feet pointed toward the back when you sit down. Women should not hand anything directly to a Buddhist monk or touch the monk or his robes in any way as doing so would violate one of his most important vows that he should not touch women.

Thai society, like many others in Asia, is very hierarchical. People earn more respect with increasing age, wealth, and education. As a general rule, a subordinate follows the directions of his or her superior without comment or question. In return, the superior takes care of the subordinate as a mentor of sorts. Thais will ask some questions concerning age, salary, and marital status to show their concern, while which may seem rude to Westerners.

Supplementary Reading: Social Customs and Etiquette of Some OBOR Countries

The social structure is often revealed in restaurants when either the oldest or the wealthiest person in the group pays for everyone. To make a good impression on your superiors and subordinates, you had better bring them small gifts, particularly after trips.

Thai people are extremely polite and their behavior is tightly controlled by etiquette, much of it based on their Buddhist religion. It is a non-confrontational society, in which public dispute or criticism is to be avoided at all costs. The Thai smile can say many things. Thais smile when they are happy, amused, embarrassed, uncertain, wrong, annoyed or furious.

In the business world, most Thais use handshaking. The traditional greeting is the *wai*, a prayer-like gesture in which the palms are pressed together and the fingers held upward with the thumbs almost touching the nose. The height to which the hands should be raised depends on the status of the person you are *waiing*. In the case of monks, dignitaries and old people the hands are raised to the bridge of the nose, with equals only as far as the chest. Social inferiors generally put their palms higher and keep their heads to a lower level than those they regard as superior. Younger people *wai* first. The *wai* is also used when saying "thank you", when receiving a gift or special favor. Young people and inferiors are not *waid*, but nodded slightly to. You would be regarded as a little foolish should you *wai* to them.

When sitting in a chair, avoid crossing your feet, as this may result in pointing your foot at someone, which is considered to be rude. The feet are the least sacred. When sitting on the floor, follow the example of your host: crossed legs are fine for men, but women usually bend their knees and tuck their feet under and to one side. The head, being the highest part of the body, is revered. Never touch a Thai person's head. Avoid touching Thai people, since it is too intimate a gesture and an invasion of personal space.

When eating a meal with Thais, try to use the correct utensils. Rice dishes are eaten with a fork and spoon only, and noodles are eaten with chopsticks. When a group of people order food in a restaurant, it is usually served "family style" with common serving platters in the middle of the table. Instead of heaping the food all at once onto your plate, follow the example of your Thai hosts: they will take a spoonful or two from the serving platter, put it next to their rice on their personal plates, then eat it slowly. Be sure to leave a little food on your plate to show that you have had enough, and never take the last bite from the common platter. And it is considered very rude to blow your nose or to lick you fingers. The right hand must be used to pick up food eaten with the fingers.

Bargaining is a common practice, and should always be employed when hiring vehicles or shopping at open-air markets. There is no bargaining in restaurants, supermarkets, or when the price is indicated on a label or sign. Tipping generally isn't necessary, especially at less expensive restaurants and for taxi rides.

Thailand's hierarchical system is not limited to social structure. It also affects personal clothing. Clothing from the lower parts of the body should never be left anywhere in a high position. This applies particularly to socks and underwear, and also to shorts and skirts. This is the case even when washing and drying clothes. Thais have two clothes lines: a high one for most clothes and a low one for underwear and socks.

Revealing clothing, such as shorts, low cut dresses and T-shirts and skimpy bathing suits, either worn by either men or women, is a little disgusting to most Thais. In temples, long trousers or skirts must be worn, and monks should on no account be touched in any way by women.

The feet, and therefore the shoes, are the lowest part of the body and are often dusty. This is why shoes are always removed when entering a home or temple, so be sure you always have clean feet or an extra pair of socks that you can put on just before reaching your destination. For this reason, most Thais wear slip-on shoes to avoid constantly tying and untying laces.

2 Laos

Laos is a landlocked country of the same size as Great Britain. It comprises mostly mountains and plateau. The Mekong River flows through western and southern regions and forms a natural border with Thailand and Myanmar. On its banks nestle most of Laos' important cities, such as the capital Vientiane.

Being a small nation, still largely undeveloped, Laos is a land of towering mountains and dense tropical forests. The vegetation is diverse and rich comprising tropical and subtropical species, from mango and palms to hardwoods. About half of the country is still covered with primary forests.

Lao villages are small. Houses are usually constructed with bamboo and are raised above the ground on wooden piles. The space beneath the house is used to store tools and to secure livestock at night. An elevated granary stands a short distance from the family's living quarters.

Supplementary Reading Social Customs and Etiquette of Some OBOR Countries

The predominant religion is Theravada Buddhism(上座部佛教). Animism(泛灵论) is common particularly among the mountain tribes. Buddhism and spirit worship coexist easily, even though *phi* worship is officially banned. The clearest example of this is the *Baci* ceremony which all lowland Laotians practice regularly at every major life event such as birth, marriage and death. The ceremony calls all the good spirits together to ward off the evil spirits and to get strength for these important moments in life. Most Christians (primarily Roman Catholic) have left since 1975.

There are some general rules of conduct that a traveler in Laos should follow. It is best to avoid the time round 11a.m. when visiting a *wat* (Buddhist temple), as this is when monks usually take their morning meal. Women should not attempt to shake the hand of a monk, hand anything to him, or sit beside him since monks are not allowed to touch women.

When sitting down, feet should point away from the altar and main image. Arms and legs should be fully covered when visiting wats. A small donation is advisable, and it is appropriate to kneel down when giving it. In general pointing with the index finger is considered rude. Patting children on the head should be avoided, as it is the most sacred part of the body. The traditional form of greeting is with hands together, prayer-like, and with head bowed, as in most parts of Asia, but handshaking is done more frequently today.

Great attention should be paid when taking photographs. One should be very wary in areas that have (or could have) military importance such as airports, where all photography is prohibited. People should be careful when photographing official functions and parades without permission, and should always ask permission before photographing in a temple.

3 Myanmar

The Burmese people call their country the Golden Land. The name may come from the Burmese custom of decorating Buddhist pagodas(宝塔) with gold leaf, which makes them glitter in the sunlight. The term may also refer to the golden glow of Burma's bountiful(丰富的) rice crop just before harvest time, for Burma grows so much rice—the basic food of much of Asia—that it exports large quantities of this grain, or it may refer to the fact that the sun shines throughout many months of the year. Whatever the reason, it is an appropriate name, for Burma is well endowed with fertile land, great forests rich in valuable wood, and important mineral resources.

After a long period of isolation, the Burmese has started to encourage tourism. Foreigners will be expected to pay several times more than locals for accommodations, domestic airfares, and entry to tourist sites.

Modern household appliances, radios, and movie theaters are now found in the cities, but most Burmese live without these luxuries. Automobiles, trucks, bicycles, and motorbikes are found on the roads.

In their daily lives, most Burmese cling to traditional values and customs. In both the rural areas and the cities, the Burmese prefer to wear traditional garments rather than Western-style clothing. Both men and women wear skirts in the Myanmar's hot climate with the exception of those in the military, who wear pants. The "skirts" that are worn are made out of *longyi*, which is a cloth that is wrapped around the body (one way for men and another way for women) and with the end slipped into the waist. Above the waist, women wear blouses, either short-sleeved or long-sleeved, while the men wear thin shirts. Since the weather is so hot, they don't wear shoes but sandals. An item used year-round is an umbrella. Umbrellas are used year-round as protection from the intensely hot sun or for protection from the rain.

A typical Burmese family lives in a bamboo house elevated on stilts. Usually there is a long porch outside where the family eats and relaxes. Rice is the basic food, and it is often taken with the fingers from a common bowl and dipped into dishes made with chicken, fish, or beef and spiced with curry powder and other seasoning.

Women have equal status with men in Burma. In the past women have ruled Burma as queens, and now they are active in politics and the professions. Women operate nearly all of the bazaar(市场、市集)stalls and shops in local markets.

4 India

India, officially the Republic of India, is a sovereign state in South Asia, where it comprises the bulk of the Indian peninsula. It is the 7th largest country in the world by land area, and the second most populous, with a population of over 1.2 billion people. Hinduism is by far the most prevalent, with almost 80% of the population describing themselves as Hindu. The main language is Hindi and English.

Indians hold their palms together and say "Namaste" (nuh-mus-tay) while greeting

Supplementary Reading Social Customs and Etiquette of Some OBOR Countries

each other. Hugging and kissing on the cheeks, especially with the opposite sex is frowned upon and should be avoided. Shoes should be taken off before entering an Indian house or a place of worship—temples, mosques, gurdwaras.

Some people might prefer to wear a traditional kurta pyjama instead of a shirt and pants. Also, some women wear a veil—whether it is the burqa or hijaab in Muslims, or a ghunghat (head drape drawn till the chin) in Hindus. Indian bobbing of the head sometimes is very confusing. A vertical nod indicates yes while a horizontal nod means no.

It is common for Indians to invite guests, business associates or friends, to their home and give them a tour of the entire house including bedrooms. When paying a visit to an Indian home, sweets or chocolates, something of not great monetary value are acceptable. Avoid wine and flowers though. Alcohol is generally frowned upon as a gift choice, and flowers are considered unusual for a gift.

Although the tradition of eating on the floor or a mat has changed, some households might still prefer to dine on the floor. Unlike the western use of spoon and fork, traditionally Indians use their hands to consume their food. If you are not comfortable with using your hands to eat, feel free to ask for cutlery. Eat whatever has been offered to you, and when the host insists on a second helping, say "yes", otherwise, they assume you do not like the food. Indian culture dictates that the left hand is unclean, and hence the right hand must be used for most activities, including eating food. Whether it is touching or eating food, paying money or giving a gift, remember to use your right hand; using your left hand would be considered offensive and rude.

Keep in mind the major dietary restrictions when it comes to Hindus, Muslims, and Sikhs in India. Hindus consider cow scared and do not eat beef, while Muslims eat beef but consider the consumption of pork to be "haraam" or a sin. Sikhs abstain from both beef and pork.

Never talk about the Indian culture in a negative light. Indians are vehemently proud of their legacy and diverse cultures. Also, refrain from getting into any religion-related topics. Religion is a sensitive issue in the country. Do not expect business meetings to start on time. In India punctuality may mean being half an hour to one hour late.

5 Greece

Greece is located at the southern end of the Balkan Peninsula. Ancient Greece, the cradle of Western civilization, was a land of small city-states whose people shared a language and a set of religious beliefs. Here, for a brief moment in the long history of humanity, men of genius, men of spirit, and men of vision lived, created, and set foundations. Words that they spoke more than 2,000 years ago are still vital and inspiring today.

Like the people of every other nation on earth, the Greeks now are a mixture of many peoples. Today, the population of Greece is near 9,000,000. There are about 3,000,000 Greeks who live outside the national borders, most of them in the United States, Australia, Germany, and Cyprus.

The majority of Greeks, in fact, are country people making their homes in small towns, villages, and hamlets. They make a meager living cultivating their fields and orchards or tending their vineyards and olive groves. Tilling the often-rocky ground is backbreaking work, but the Greek farmer is attached to the land. He loves the earth, and the smallest patch of arable land is under cultivation.

Over 90 percent of the population belongs to the Greek Orthodox Church. The black-robed, longhaired, and bearded papas is a familiar and important figure in villages and towns all over the country. He officiates at weddings, baptisms, and funerals. He celebrates the name day of every important patron saint, arranges processions, blesses the livestock and the crops, presides over church festivals, and occasionally is still called on to drive out a demon.

Easter is one of the most important holidays in the Greek Orthodox calendar, and it is celebrated with great pomp. Christmas, though also an official holiday, means less to the religious feelings of the Greeks. Between Christmas and New Year's Day the children sing carols from house to house, collecting pennies and bits of food. Epiphany, commemorating Christ's baptism in the Jordan River, is celebrated on January 6th.

The basis of all Greek life is the family, and family bonds are very strong. The Greeks openly show their love for their children, especially the boys.

Greece is a country of strong traditions. Despite (or maybe thanks to) its turbulent history marked by numerous foreign occupations, the sense of "Greekness" is strongly embedded in the minds and habits of the Greek people, and customs and traditions are strongly alive in the daily lives of people. You might find it hard to believe when you observe young Athenians whose idea of a good night out is a pizza dinner followed by dancing and drinking cocktails in trendy seaside nightclubs that have little to do with traditional Greece, but that's only the surface. They will dance to the captivating rhythms of

Supplementary Reading Social Customs and Etiquette of Some OBOR Countries

the typical Greek music, know the lyrics of traditional songs (and sing along) and observe all national customs and traditions just like their parents, grandparents and generations did.

The people of Greece are a hearty collection, and live in a land sharply divided into two ways of life: the traditional life and the urban/ tourist life. As a result, two very different cultures have developed just in the past half-century, each with its own subtleties and nuances.

Greeks have a few mannerisms that differ from those in the Western world. Most important are the head gestures for an affirmative or negative. A Greek will nod as yes, the same way as a Westerner would, a downward tilt of the head, but a Greek will indicate no by an upward tilt, not a side to side shake. In general, Greeks are very physical people. Upon meeting it is not unusual for Greeks to kiss each other on both cheeks if they are acquainted. Meeting for the first time men expect a firm and hearty handshake. Do not let yourself be perceived as feeble. Offensive gestures include the sign of the fig (a closed fist, thumb between pointer and middle fingers and directed at someone) and the horns (a fist, pointer and pinky fingers extended). One gesture that should not be done is to extend your arm and hold up all 5 fingers at someone (like to denote the number "5", for example). Do not do this because it denotes hostility, disrespect, and loathing. It is a remnant of the Nazi salute.

The Greek mentality is that of great pride and honor: pride in their past and pride in the survival of their way of life under centuries of occupation. This also gives the Greeks a great deal of competitiveness. Sometimes, this pride works to their detriment, and Greeks may act out of ego rather than logic. The most apparent display of this is the Greek road. Athens has been called one of the craziest cities in Europe to drive in by governments and tourists alike, partly due to poor city planning, and partly to the tendency of Greeks to use the horn over the brake.

The Greeks love to eat. Eating is a social event in Greece and one must truly appreciate a hearty Greek meal in the company of family or friends. Breakfast is usually light, bread with some olives, olive oil, cheese and perhaps some coffee and juice. Lunch is the major meal of the day, eaten anywhere between noon and 2 p.m. Dinner is lighter, and usually fairly late in the evening.

If a Greek invites you out for a dinner or a drink, don't EVER try to make him "split the bill in half" as people often do in Northern Europe. Some tourists want to be nice to their host for the evening, and they snap the bill out of his hand and pay it. The Greek man will be more embarrassed than you could ever imagine and friendship is close to be ruined in such occasion!

If you are invited to a Greek home, remember to bring something for the host. Flowers or chocolates are the most common gifts. If the occasion is a Name Day, you must bring a present, which you should deliver when you enter the house. The present will be put together with the rest of the presents on a table unopened. The Greeks will open the gifts when all the guests have left.

Even if it says everywhere that tips are included in the price, it is common to give tips if you're satisfied with the service. About 10% would be appropriate. But remember not to "over-tip", something that this little story explains well: Some friends wanted to tip the waiter at the hotel where they had stayed for 2 weeks, so they left 30 Euro the last evening. When they were 10 steps away from their table the waiter stood in front of them saying that they had mistaken the Greek money. They explained that they hadn't. The waiter then joined them in the bar, where they had coffee and Metaxa, and later, drinks and ouzos. When they called the barman for the bill, they found out that the waiter they had tipped before already paid the bill, which was much higher than 30 Euros.

6 Israel

The nation of Israel, which was established in 1948, is one of the smallest countries of the world. But despite its size, Israel's early years were filled with great accomplishments in the face of many difficulties. The country increased its agricultural and industrial production by several times, and absorbed hundreds of thousands of new immigrants.

Israeli society is the most democratic in the Middle East. Its press is free except for censorship of military operations. There are strong opposition political parties and freely expressed public criticism of the government. There is a strong feeling for social and political equality and the gap between rich and poor is less than that in most countries.

Israelis lead a varied life. They dress very much like Europeans or Americans, but with emphasis on informal styles. At one time open-necked khaki(卡其布) shirts and shorts were nearly a uniform for men. Now full-length trousers have replaced the shorts, although the open-necked shirt is still common, even among men attending formal functions. On the other hand, some Israeli women have become very style-conscious. Nearly every newspaper runs a

Supplementary Reading Social Customs and Etiquette of Some OBOR Countries

fashion page with pictures of clothes manufactured in Israel that can compete with the most fashionable New York and Paris styles. The average woman, however, dresses quite practically, as required by her work at home, on the farm, in the office, or in a factory.

There are some special customs and etiquette in Israel. A warm handshake followed by "Shalom" is the acceptable form of greeting when you meet and depart. Titles are not considered important. They prefer to address others by the first name. Being punctual is important, but Israelis are casual about time, and it is not unusual for your associates to be late for up to half an hour. To impress your host, have your business cards engraved. It is a sign of status in Israel. Business is conducted at a similar pace to that of a large American city such as New York. Decision-making takes more time than in the West. Top executives make the final decisions in private companies. Companies owned by a group of people make decisions collectively. Do not photograph altercations between Jews and Arabs.

There are ten etiquette of hajj(朝圣). These are as follows:

(1) requite all wrongdoings and satisfy all adversaries;

(2) make provision for hajj from one's lawful wealth;

(3) learn the pillars of hajj and its ceremonies;

(4) be kind and forbearing with others, lest the reward be nullified;

(5) observe the obligations of prayers and its statutes;

(6) be open-handed, maintain the poor and spend as much as he/she is able to;

(7) at the station of "Arafat", remember the Day of Judgment (*Yawmil Qiamat*);

(8) should not miss visitation of the Prophet's (S) grave in *Madinah*;

(9) after return from hajj, one should turn toward *Akhirat* (Hereafter);

(10) one should remember his parents and other close relatives who have passed away with pious prayers and make up for them if they could not fulfill their obligations for hajj.

7 Russia

The Russian Federation has gone through many changes in recent years, as communism ended in 1991. At that time, the U.S.S.R. as it was called separated into 10 plus independent states. This separation ended the communism reign that had lasted from 1917 to 1991.

Foreign businessmen are expected to be on time to all business appointments. However, the Russian counterpart may be not punctual, and usually will not make apology for lateness.

Social events are more relaxed. It is acceptable for foreigners to be 15 to 30 minutes late.

The business lunch or dinner is generally the time to seal a deal, not to make decisions, negotiate, or get to know each other. Usually the one who makes the invitation pays the bill, although the guest is expected to make an effort to pay. Sometimes other circumstances determine the payee (such as rank). There is no need to give extra tips for dining.

If attending dinner at a family residence, it is appropriate to bring a gift, such as a bottle of wine, desserts, or a bouquet of flowers. You might need to remove your shoes before entering a Russian home. And allow the more senior members of your party to enter rooms ahead of you and the seating arrangement is usually predetermined.

When shaking hands with someone, be sure to take off your gloves, as it is considered rude if not to. Be alert and open to taking a drink or having a toast, as refusing to do so is a serious breach of etiquette. Give in coats and large bags when entering theatres, restaurants, museums etc.

Businessmen in Russia usually wear suits that are dark and well tailored along with good dress shoes. A businessman's wardrobe demonstrates the individual's image as a professional. Men often do not take off their jackets in negotiations. Do not stand with your hands in your pockets. This is considered rude. Women dress rather conservatively, avoiding overly flashy or gaudy outfits. Women should always cover their heads when entering into any Russian Orthodox Churches. Skirts rather than pants should be worn. When attending dinner in a citizen's home, casual dress of slacks and a nice shirt without a tie are appropriate.

8 Poland

Though the Polish people have struggled over the centuries to keep hold of their territory, Polish culture is rich with customs and tradition because Poles have been too stubborn to let history's vagaries quash or dilute (冲淡) their identity. Getting to know the follwing customs will help a lot when travelling in Poland.

Bring a bouquet of flowers if you are invited into someone's home. Shake hands when you greet people (both men and women), and opt for the formal greeting when addressing someone, unless you know someone or have mutually agreed on using first names. Poles love to drink. They often drink late into the night. Catholic conservatism dictates the way many Poles think, so be careful not to offend people by expressing strong religious views that

Supplementary Reading Social Customs and Etiquette of Some OBOR Countries

may run counter to tradition. In other words, keep your atheism(无神论) to yourself. If you visit a church, take off your hat. Don't make fun of the Poles!

The eating pattern for most Poles is four meals a day. Breakfast is eaten before work. A second breakfast is eaten at work around 11:00 a.m., usually just a sandwich taken from home. Dinner, the main meal of the day, is eaten around 3:00 or 4:00 p.m. It usually includes a first course of soup and a hot plate of meat, potatoes and some vegetables (beets or cabbage are common). Supper is eaten around at 7:00 p.m. It is usually a cold meal, bread, cheese, ham, cucumbers or tomatoes (in season). The office hours for most Polish workers are 7:00 a.m. to 3:00 p.m. A fruit drink is often served with dinner and coffee or tea is served with the other meals. Most of the Polish people are Roman Catholic. Fridays are still meatless for much of the population, even when meat is available.

The Catholic faith also gives cause for many celebrations, such as Christmas and Easter feasts, and baptism and wedding gatherings, for which traditional food have evolved. Keep both of your hands above the table while you're eating.

In Poland, Easter is the happiest day of the year, when the Catholic Church celebrates the resurrection of Christ. The Poles have always kept the fasting period during the six weeks preceding Easter. Eggs are a major item of the Easter celebration. Throughout Poland, during the week before Easter, housewives are busy with spring cleaning and preparing many dishes that will grace Easter morning tables.

On Good Friday, the eggs are decorated. Some of the eggs are dyed in water in which yellow-onion skins, red-onion skins or beet peelings are boiled. Others are covered with intricate designs using beeswax and bright-colored paints. Saturday is the day to complete preparations for Sunday's breakfast. Decorated baskets are filled with hard-cooked eggs, cold cuts, sausage, wheat bread, slices of babka (cake-like sweet bread) and mazurka (a rich pastry) and a small lamb (the symbol of Jesus) made of butter. The baskets are taken to church to be blessed.

There is something special about Christmas Eve in Poland. This joyous, emotional dinner celebration unites separated families and renews friendships that are often strained by the trying conditions of everyday life. Each year there is an extra place set at the Christmas Eve dinner table. A lighted candle is in the window facing the street. The candle flickers through the darkness in the hope that Christ, in the form of a stranger, will join the family for dinner. It may also serve as a beacon to help guide the spirit of any family member who could not travel the distance in person. As a reminder of Christ's humble birthplace, a handful of straw is placed beneath the traditional white-linen tablecloth. Before the meal begins, a prayer of thanks is given. Slim wafers or pieces of unleavened bread similar to communion hosts, impressed with biblical figures of Christ, angels, lambs or Blessed Mary, are passed to each participant. Several wafers are then taken to the barn and fed to the family livestock. Other blessed wafers have already been mailed to far-away relatives and friends.

No meat is served during Christmas Eve dinner. Christmas Eve is a time of strict fasting, and the closing hours of a four-week period of penance called Advent. Although dinner is meatless, it doesn't mean the meal isn't a feast. It begins with at least three different kinds of soups, including meatless borscht, closely followed by three traditional fish entrees of which at least two are carp and pike. Borscht, a bright red Polish and Russian soup, was originally made with cow parsnip.

9 Romania

Romania is situated in the southeastern part of Central Europe and shares borders with Hungary to the northwest, Serbia to the southwest, Bulgaria to the south, the Black Sea and Ukraine to the southeast and to the north and the Republic of Moldova to the east. Roughly the size of Oregon, Romania is the second largest country in the East Europe, after Poland.

Romania's territory features splendid mountains, beautiful rolling hills, fertile plains and numerous rivers and lakes. The Carpathian Mountains traverse the center of the country bordered on both sides by foothills and finally the great plains of the outer rim. Forests cover over one quarter of the country and the fauna is one of the richest in Europe including bears, deer, lynx, chamois and wolves. The legendary Danube River ends its eight-country journey through eight European countries at the Black Sea by forming one of the biggest and most interesting wetlands in the world, the Danube Delta.

Romania is full of interesting customs and traditions. Essentially sedentary and strongly aware of their continuity, the Romanian people created during the centuries their own folk culture crystallized in a unitary system.

Romanians are very friendly and hospitable, with an innate sense of humor. Older Romanian people particularly appreciate old-fashioned politeness. It is respectful to use Mrs. or Mr. when using the name of a person that you firstly meet. Handshaking is the most common form of greeting. When a Romanian man is introduced to a woman, he will

Supplementary Reading: Social Customs and Etiquette of Some OBOR Countries

probably kiss her hand, strictly avoiding her eyes. If one refuses what a host offers to eat or drink, this will often be taken as a polite refusal by guest who really means to say "yes". If you want to really refuse the offer find a polite excuse and say it firmly or ask for a replacement. It is common to linger once the meal (lunch or dinner) is over.

When visiting a Romanian home, bring a small gift. Most common gifts include flowers or chocolate (for women only), a bottle of wine or liquor. The number of flowers that one offers must always be odd. Other well-appreciated gifts include Western cosmetics (i.e. after-shave) and clothing. All gifts should be wrapped, but many Romanians might not unwrap their gifts in your presence.

Most Romanians prefer to live a life at more relaxed pace as people in many Latin countries do. Although casual dress is fine in most occasions, wearing a suit and tie, or the women's equivalent, is important at business meetings. Appointments are necessary and punctuality is expected. It is acceptable to ask a person's age, politics, income or religion.

References

[1] Axtell R. E. Gestures: the Do's and Taboos of Body Language Around the World [M]. New York: Wiley, 1998

[2] Brown R, Ford M. Address in American English[J]. Journal of Abnormal & Social Psychology, 1961, 62(2):375-385.

[3] Brown P B. Politeness: Some Universals in Language Usage [J]. Cambridge University Press, 1987, 42(1):135-135.

[4] Burgoon J. K., Buller D. B., Woodall, W. G. Nonverbal communication: The unspoken dialogue (2nd ed.)[M]. New York: McGraw-Hill, 1996.

[5] Duckling L. A Dictionary of Epithets and Terms of Address[M]. London and New York: Routledge, 1990.

[6] Edward T. H., Mildred R. H. The Hidden Differences: Doing Business with the Japanese[M]. New York: Anchor Books Editions,1987

[7] Goffman E. Interaction Ritual: Essays on Face-to-face Interaction [J]. American Journal of Sociology, 1967, 33(3):462.

[8] Knapp M, Wiemann J M, Daly J A. Nonverbal Communication: Issues and Appraisal [J]. Human Communication Research, 2010, 4(3):271-280.

[9] Kluckhohn, C. Values and Value-orientations in the Theory of Action: An Exploration in Definition and Classification. In: Parsons, T. and Shils, E., Eds., Toward a General Theory of Action[M]. Cambridge, MA: Harvard University Press, 1951

[10] Javidi A, Javidi M. Cross-cultural Analysis of Interpersonal Bonding: A look at East and West[J]. Howard Journal of Communications, 1991, 3(1-2):129-138.

[11] Leathers, D. G. Successful Nonverbal Communication: Principles and Applications [M]. New York: Macmillan, 1986.

[12] Rokeach, M. The Nature of Human Values, New York:The Free Press,1973.

[13] Ruesch J, Kees W. Nonverbal Communication: Notes on the Visual Perception of Human Relations [M] Berkeley: The University of California Press, 1956.

[14] Samovar L. A., Porter R. E. Intercultural Communication: A Reader [M]. Belmont,

Calif: Wadsworth Publishing Co., 1982.

[15] Schwartz S. H., Bilsky W. Toward a Universal Psychological Structure of Human Values[J]. Journal of Personality & Social Psychology, 1987, 53(3):550-562.

[16] Todd R. Armstrong, Intercultural Communication[M]. London: SAGE Publications Ltd, 2008.

[17] Widdowson, H. G. Teaching Language as Communication[M]. Shanghai: Shanghai Foreign Language Education Press, 1999.

[18] Yum, J. O. The Impact of Confucianism on Interpersonal Relationships and Communication Patterns in East Asia[M]. Intercultural Communication: A Reader (7th edition). Belmont, Calif.: Wadsworth Publishing Co., 1994.

[19] 毕继万. 跨文化非言语交际[M]. 北京:外语教学与研究出版社,1999.

[20] 蔡荣寿. 跨文化交际通论[M]. 苏州:苏州大学出版社, 2009.

[21] 陈晨. 从跨文化角度对比英汉称赞语和答语[C]. 汉语言文化研究. 广西:广西师范大学出版社,1996.

[22] 窦卫霖. 跨文化交际基础[M]. 北京:对外经济贸易大学出版社, 2010.

[23] 杜学增. 中英(英语国家)文化习俗比较[M]. 北京:外语与教学出版社, 2010.

[24] 董小川. 儒家文化与美国基督教文化[M]. 北京:商务印书馆,1999.

[25] 耿二岭. 体态语概说[M]. 北京:北京语言学院出版社,1988.

[26] 何自然. 语用学与英语学习[M]. 上海:上海外语教育出版社,1997.

[27] 塞缪尔·亨廷顿,劳伦斯·哈里森. 文化的重要作用——价值观如何影响人类进步[M]. 北京:新华出版社, 2002.

[28] 洪晓楠. 当代中国文化哲学研究[M]. 大连:大连出版社, 2001.

[29] 胡超. 跨文化交际实用教程[M]. 北京:外语教学与研究出版社, 2006.

[30] 胡文仲. 跨文化交际学概论[M]. 北京:外语教学与研究出版社, 1999.

[31] 胡文仲. 超越文化的屏障[M]. 北京:外语教学与研究出版社,2002.

[32] 黄永红. 跨文化交际学教程[M]. 武汉:华中科技大学出版社, 2010.

[33] 黄育才. 跨文化交际实用英语教程[M]. 上海:复旦大学出版社, 2015.

[34] 贾玉新. 跨文化交际学[M]. 上海:上海外语教育出版社, 1997.

[35] 孟小平. 体态与交际[M]. 北京:北京语言学院出版社, 1988.

[36] 莫爱屏. 跨文化交际教程[M]. 北京:北京大学出版社, 2016.

[37] 石应平. 中外民俗概论[M]. 成都:四川大学出版社, 2002.

[38] 王力. 中国语法理论[M]. 北京:中华书局, 1954

[39] 夏基松. 现代西方哲学教程[M]. 上海:上海人民出版社, 2005.

[40] 许志伟,赵敦华. 冲突与互补:基督教哲学在中国[M]. 北京:社会科学文献出版社,2000.

[41] 杨峰. 跨文化交际[M]. 武汉:武汉理工大学出版社,2010.

[42] 庄恩平,Nan M. Sussman. 跨文化沟通[M]. 北京:外语教学与研究出版社,2014.

[43] 赵序,金丽娟. 中外民俗[M]. 天津:天津大学出版社,2011.

[44] 张玉立,陈珞瑜. 中西民俗对比研究[M]. 北京:中国社会科学出版社,2016.

[45] 朱永涛,王立礼. 英语国家社会与文化入门[M]. 北京:高等教育出版社,2005.

[46] http://www.chinesefolklore.org.cn/web/index.php?NewsID=7944

[47] https://www.wikihow.com/Avoid-Etiquette-Mistakes-in-Japan

[48] https://www.wikihow.com/Greet-in-Islam

[49] https://www.modern-manners-and-etiquette.com/business-dining-etiquette.html

[50] https://www.etiquettescholar.com/dining_etiquette/business_etiquette.html

[51] https://globaledge.msu.edu/

[52] https://www.etiquettescholar.com/index.html

[53] https://www.travelchinaguide.com/essential/etiquette.htm

[54] https://www.britannica.com/place/Spain

[55] https://smallbusiness.chron.com/etiquette-business-introductions-2912.html

[56] http://www.a-to-z-of-manners-and-etiquette.com/international-etiquette.html

[57] Susie, W. Intercultural Communication and International Business Etiquette, https://www.linkedin.com/pulse/probe-international-business-susie-wilson,2014